# We Shall Be Changed

# We Shall Be Changed

## Questions for the Post-Pandemic Church

Edited by

## Mark D. W. Edington

CHURCH
PUBLISHING
INCORPORATED

Church Publishing
19 East 34th Street
New York, NY 10016
www.churchpublishing.org

Cover design by Jennifer Kopec, 2Pug Design
Typeset by PerfecType, Nashville, Tennessee

A record of this book is available from the Library of Congress.

ISBN-13: 978-1-64065-372-6 (paperback)
ISBN-13: 978-1-64065-373-3 (ebook)

# CONTENTS

# CONTENTS

*We thought we had the answers*
*It was the questions we had wrong*

—U2, "11 O'Clock Tick Tock"

Preface

# The Breath of the Spirit and the Winds of Change

ON JANUARY 23, 2020, the city of Wuhan, China was effectively closed off from the world by local authorities in an effort to arrest the exponential spread of a virus not previously identified in humans. Seven days later, on January 30, the World Health Organization declared the outbreak of the virus a "Public Health Emergency of International Concern"; in the previous ten days, the number of reported cases in Wuhan had grown from 282 to 7,800.[1]

On March 11, what was now identified as the 2019 novel coronavirus (2019-nCoV) was declared a pandemic; on that day, only four nations outside of China (Italy, Saudi Arabia, Mongolia, and Qatar) had instituted lockdowns in an effort to control the spread of the disease. By the first week of April, more than half the world's population—3.9 billion people—were living under public orders limiting their movement, activities, and social lives, an experience arguably without precedent in all of human history.[2]

---

1. "How Bad Will It Get?" (leader article), *The Economist*, February 1–7, 2020, 9.
2. Alasdair Sandford, "Coronavirus: Half of Humanity Now on Lockdown as 90 Countries Call for Confinement," *Euronews*, April 3, 2020, https:// www.euronews.com/2020/04/02/coronavirus-in-europe-spain-s-death-toll -hits-10-000-after-record-950-new-deaths-in-24-hou

# PREFACE

Now known as the Severe Acute Respiratory Syndrome Coronavirus 2 (SARS-CoV-2), the disease is highly transmissible between humans, largely because no virus has previously appeared among us that would have stimulated the creation of a natural immune response. As of the day I write these lines, 22,959,813 cases have been diagnosed worldwide, with 5,623,990 of those cases appearing in the United States; said in different terms, the United States has seen 24.9% of all diagnosed cases of the virus, while having 4.3% of the world's people.[3]

Nearly eight hundred thousand people have died of Covid-19, the disease caused by the virus; of those, 175,409 have died in the United States so far. To set that in perspective, it is as though the entire population of Salem, Oregon or Providence, Rhode Island had died.

Covid-19 is deadly to a relatively small number of those whom it infects, but the way in which it is deadly is indicated in the name of the virus itself: severe, acute, respiratory. The onset of the disease process is swift and sudden; it is very serious, even quickly catastrophic; and it centers on the respiratory system, causing its victims, in essence, to suffocate.

On May 25, 2020, George Floyd was arrested in the Powderhorn Park neighborhood of Minneapolis after allegedly passing a counterfeit twenty-dollar bill at a convenience store. He was approached by two police officers from the Minneapolis Police Department while sitting in a car near the store, ordered to leave his vehicle, and handcuffed.

---

3. Coronavirus Resource Center, Center for Systems Science and Engineering, Johns Hopkins University, "Covid-19 Dashboard," https://coronavirus.jhu.edu/map.html; "World Population," https://en.wikipedia.org/wiki/World_population

Two other police officers then arrived at the scene. According to the criminal complaint filed against one of those officers for murder in the second and third degree, Floyd was compliant with the officers while being interviewed but resisted entering the squad car. In the ensuing struggle, the officers placed the still-handcuffed Floyd face-down on the sidewalk, and one of them "placed his left knee in the area of Mr. Floyd's head and neck."

"Mr. Floyd said, 'I can't breathe' multiple times," the complaint adds.[4]

---

The breath is being taken away from us. That is both the physical and the spiritual implication of this year of pandemics. It is not just a virus that attacks our lungs' ability to supply oxygen to our bodies; it is not just a uniformed knee that saps the breath from the lungs of a Black man. It is what has been revealed about our society and our culture by the catalyzing force of two simultaneous pandemics linked by the deprivation of breath.

Covid-19 attacks its victims by degrading the capacity of their lungs to do the essential work of oxygenating blood. But in responding to the disease, in dealing with—or denying the significance of—the pleas of qualified, scientifically trained public health professionals to adopt simple measures in order to protect the health of others, Covid has dramatically revealed our society as one already suffocating. For decades,

---

4. State of Minnesota, County of Hennepin, Criminal Complaint against Derek Michael Chauvin, Court File 27-CR-20-12646, May 29, 2020, https://www.hennepinattorney.org/-/media/Attorney/Derek-Chauvin-Criminal-Complaint.pdf

it has been gradually, chronically deprived of the necessary oxygen of common purpose, a sense of shared destiny, a feeling of responsibility toward the neighbor and the other. The refusal to wear masks or to abide by social distancing is not so much a political statement as a refusal to accept a basic minimum of responsibility for the well-being of others. It is the morality of solipsism. Nothing could be less Christian.

For four hundred years, American society and culture has been in some fundamental way premised on controlling the breath of those whose skin appears not to be white. It has insisted on the ability to control bodies of color—often using the subtle tools of controlling and calibrating access to institutions of education or structures of economic and political power, but when somehow thought necessary by strangling the breath of life, either by the knee or the noose. In *The Fire Next Time,* James Baldwin proposed a link between race, death, and state power in the United States:

> Perhaps the whole root of our trouble, the human trouble, is that we will sacrifice all the beauty of our lives, will imprison ourselves in totems, taboos, crosses, blood sacrifices, steeples, mosques, races, armies, flags, nations in order to deny the fact of death, which is the only fact we have. It seems to me that one ought to rejoice in the *fact* of death—ought to decide, indeed, to earn one's death by confronting with passion the conundrum of life. . . . But white Americans do not believe in death, and this is why the darkness of my skin so intimidates them.[5]

5. James Baldwin, *The Fire Next Time* (New York: Vintage Books, 1993), 91–92; emphasis original. Quoted in James Martel, *Unburied Bodies: Subversive Corpses and the Authority of the Dead* (Amherst, Mass.: Amherst College Press, 2018), 99.

Baldwin's perceptive claim is that the power insisted upon by white Americans over communities of color is linked to an imagined power over death; and this is why, in his analysis, lives of color are somehow seen as legitimately controlled, expended, abused, enslaved, or ended by the power of the state. And it is why the idea of giving up that power causes a reaction of such desperation; for to do so would require the white community to confront the unyielding power of death on its own terms. Communities of color have had no choice in the matter; a full and unflinching confrontation with death has never been thought a choice, and has therefore been embraced in cultural expression. It is not coincidental that in describing the enduring significance of the "Sorrow Songs" in the cultural development of enslaved Americans, W. E. B. Dubois called one such song "the cradle song of death which all men know."[6]

Here is where, for the church and the claims of the gospel, our two pandemics converge. The pandemic of white supremacy has been revealed in these months as the long-nurtured and ill-founded desire of the white community to use state power as a way of casting the shadow of death entirely on another community—in this case, one defined by race. Simultaneously, the public health crisis of Covid-19 has shattered in a single moment the idea that such a defense, however subconsciously supported and legally enacted, could ever achieve its end. If our original sin is the creation of unjust systems of power, if our motive in doing so is to seek somehow to blunt the sting of death by shifting it onto a community kept powerless for the purpose, this

---

6. Du Bois speaks here of "Swing Low, Sweet Chariot." W. E. B. Du Bois, "The Sorrow Songs," in *The Souls of Black Folk* (Mineola, NY: Dover Thrift Editions, 1994), 158.

single moment has torn back the veil on both the injustice and the impossibility of our feeble effort to control what is beyond our power.

What has been revealed about our society by the nation's feckless response to the Covid-19 pandemic is the broader social disease that results from such a phantasm. If it had seemed possible somehow to liberate ourselves from the shadow of death by employing state power to control the bodies of others, then surely it is not surprising that we refuse to accept the authority of that same power to control ourselves in ways that might protect others from the potential death of infection. The refusal to wear a mask is the last protest of a culture of state power that insists upon its ability to set its own terms in contending with mortality. We have lost our sense of obligation to each other; we seek only our own dignity, our own truth, our own life, our own salvation.

It might be observed that if we were truly people of faith—if we genuinely believed in the promise of redemption and resurrection in Christ—we could then summon the courage to let go all of the pretense of a power wrongly constructed to shift death's burden onto a scapegoat category of humanity. If we truly believed that death no longer held power over us, then we would no longer feel the depth of urgency to create systems of power and control that would cast all its collective weight onto the necks of a single category of fellow-humans.

Perhaps this is the mission call of the Christian church today. If the church, wherever it exists, has itself aided and abetted the idea of the supremacy of one race over another, if it has too easily sought the embrace of state power out of a lapse of belief and a longing for more tangible protection against the power of death, then it has failed to live by what it proclaims—that the victory over death has already been won. Yet it is exactly that victory that both demands and enables the gospel's central moral claim for the conduct of life in human community—the insistence that we all stand equal before the throne of a loving God, equal in capacity for error, equal in need for redemption, and equal in dignity and possibility. As soon as we start imagining the state's power can somehow offer us a protection against death in the here and now, we have given up our faith in God's promises—here and hereafter.

This moment of pandemic has therefore made our moment one of unparalleled urgency for the Christian message; for it is only the victory of the Cross over death and the grave that can finally liberate us from constructing inequalities and supremacies that seek the false promise of protection from fears already defeated. And this means that the church is being confronted as never before with a decisive question: Will we, or will we not, proclaim that message not just in words but in actions, not just in declarations but in decisions?

---

The answer to this question is not immediately evident. Beyond any question, the long months of closure and isolation, of shuttered churches and virtual communities, set before us the certainty of change. We shall be changed. But that is the only thing that is certain.

We do not yet have answers to the question of how the church shall be changed by this pandemic year. We are not yet able to say with certainty what the implications will be of a moment in which the people to whom the angels declare "do not be afraid" have been conditioned to be fearful of each other. We cannot say what a long practice of "attending from home" will mean to churches that try to gather their flocks. There is much we cannot yet discern.

But we can begin now to glimpse the outlines of the questions that will guide our efforts to follow God's call in mission toward a more just society and a deeper sense of God's presence in our lives. Opportunities have been set before us to shake loose the systems and structures that cannot get us to where God invites us now to go, that answered a different set of needs for a different time.

In early May of 2020, as the extent of the Covid-19 impact on the life of the church became inescapable, I began to ask colleagues and friends wiser than me what questions they were grappling with as they thought about how the pandemic would shape us. The more of these conversations I pursued, the more I sensed that the questions were sorting themselves into a set of fairly clear categories:

- *Distancing and Deepening.* How might we turn this time of distancing into a time of deeper spirituality—and how might we keep that deeper conversation with God in the regathered church? How might the virtual inform—or be—the actual future of the church?

- *Liturgy and Longing.* What have we learned about the worship we have been offering from having to create new ways of worship? Are there ideas or themes we should be careful not to lose?

- *Hard Choices and Helping Hands.* What questions about financial structures and sustainability will emerge from this time of isolation to confront parishes and judicatories? Is self-help the only option?

- *Inequality, Marginalization—and Renewal.* How can we address constructively the inequality in access to resources within the church laid bare by the variety of responses to the

Covid pandemic? What responsibility do well-resourced communities and institutions have in helping poor and marginalized churches keep their communities tended and gathered?

- *Leadership—Challenge and Change.* What has the Covid pandemic taught us about the leaders and structures we have—and the leaders and structures we need?

The more I spoke with smart people about these things, the more I wanted to speak with others and the greater became my eagerness to share with a wider audience what had been shared with me. I am grateful to Nancy Bryan of Church Publishing for so eagerly embracing the idea of collecting the thoughts of these wise people into a small collection, gathered with the simple hope of guiding thought, prayer, and action as we emerge blinking from the darkness of pandemic into the light of a world God has prepared for us to remake.

But my deepest gratitude goes to the many colleagues who willingly took time in the middle of the unyielding demands of an ongoing crisis to share, without compensation, their thoughts with me—and with you. As the pattern of questions began to emerge, I sent to each of them a question that I hoped especially to draw them out on; you now have in your hands a series of five conversations engaging small groups of writers gathered around those questions. They have taken the time to write under the worst conditions and in the most demanding hours. I give thanks to God that such people have been called to exercise leadership in a moment of such difficulty.

The epigram with which this book opens states in inversion its purpose, and of the conversations it hopes to spark. Too often in its history the church has erred by insisting on its answers. We shall meet the moment of uncertainty before us only by correctly discerning the questions. These wise and prayerful people have made the best beginning of that I know.

—Mark D. W. Edington
Paris, France
The Feast of Jonathan Myrick Daniels, Seminarian and Martyr

# First Conversation: Distancing and Deepening

*How might we turn this time of distancing into a time of deeper spirituality—and how might we keep that deeper conversation with God in the regathered church? How might the virtual inform—or be—the actual future of the church?*

Paul-Gordon Chandler, Shane Claiborne,
Lorenzo Lebrija, and Greg Garrett

1

# 1

# Into the Virtual

## Paul-Gordon Chandler

"[W]E WILL ALL be changed, in a moment, in the twinkling of an eye . . ." is how St. Paul imaginatively describes our spiritual future. They are words that also poignantly define our recent experience and present reality. Almost overnight, the church's witness and worship has been turned upside down, through no choice of our own. And whether we like it or not, it is also being turned inside out. The question is quite simply whether the church will be able to adapt—not just for its survival, but with a spiritual vision to thrive in this unexplored terrain.

The words of the English seer-poet William Blake speak to our current plight: "We are led to Believe a Lie / When we see not Thro' the Eye." Fresh spiritual sight is needed to navigate this newly assigned mission. We need the ability to see "Thro' the Eye," in other words, to see God's perspective and vision. We must learn how to be led by God anew, as the Israelites of old had to learn in the wilderness.

While this journey presents its challenges, they are far outweighed by its opportunities. I am reminded of those two proverbial

3

individuals in a small cell looking out the same little window; one sees bars, and one sees stars. One sees bars, those metallic reminders of reality. One sees stars, beyond the obvious, envisaging a new future of what can be.

While many may wish to return to the way things were before this crisis, that is a wish to live in the past. How we embrace the present determines whether the church continues its demise, albeit now more quickly than before, or if she enters into what can be an unanticipated renaissance, arising out of these pandemical ashes.

Looking toward the horizon, the church's new world will require a creative embrace of technology and new media—not as substitutes, but as inspired and strategic vehicles of ministry and mission. While we are already awash with jeremiads by some within the church warning of the supposed inherent dangers of technology, it is already clear that the church's experiences in the "virtual world" have provided many parishes and ministries an opportunity to engage with a far greater number of people, providing a glimpse of the potential. Indeed, for some churches it has already shown itself to be transformational.

We are being presented with a "how," not an "if," as to the church's engagement with this new medium. Long ago a wise old sage challenged me not to focus on the breadth of ministry, but to focus on the depth and let God take care of the breadth. There is a sense that in the world of technology, if it is spiritual depth that is truly on offer, the breadth naturally flows from there, in this "like+share" social media world. Spiritual depth—the depth of what we offer—will determine the breadth—the reach of our impact.

The exciting opportunity before us in this new world of the "virtual" is to discover most effectively how to facilitate through it a genuine encounter with the Sacred, the Transcendent, through an experience of the sacramental. In so doing, the "virtual" ceases to be virtual and instead becomes a means for real spiritual transformation.

As we venture forth into this new space, it is critical that we ask again key questions that all too often have had assumed answers.

*What is the church?* During the pandemic, people have worshiped from home with others across the country, even around the world. The universal church has become a local reality. We are being forced to broaden our understanding of the church in terms of its "boundaries"—geographically, yes, but also as to how we "do and be" the church. The pandemic has led us to think again about how one prays and experiences God "always and everywhere," as opposed to primarily in the confines of a sacred place with others in corporate worship. We have become borderless in the fullest sense of the word. It has been like a miniseries of "Faith Unleashed." Our concept of the church community is even being reassessed, as through these "virtual" experiences we have been reminded that God's mission is much more about people than place. In this new world, the church comes to the people, and it must be willing to change much of the "culture" associated with church. At the same time, we need to focus this new medium on enhancing genuine community, which is essential to followers of Christ—and is too often the church's best-kept secret.

*What new skills do clergy need?* A quick surf through the proliferation of live-streaming or recorded worship services quickly separates those individuals and churches who have naturally been able to adapt and effectively facilitate for participants an encounter with the Sacred in world of the virtual, from those who could not. What does this say for the future training of our clergy? How do we teach anew the fundamental skill of storytelling that is the task of teachers of the faith?

5

*Are we effectively communicating our faith?* Communicating in this new medium toward spiritual ends requires new formats and content often unfamiliar to the church. The church will need "content creators" able to develop twenty-first-century virtual experiences that lead toward deeper spirituality, while simultaneously serving to grow the local church community.

*How do we stay a sacramental church?* One of the greatest challenges that Episcopal and Anglican churches have faced during the closure relates to celebrating Holy Communion, with the vast majority opting for Morning Prayer or some other form of liturgy. How does or doesn't the church enable its people, and all people, to experience the sacramental in a virtual medium? What else might we do?

To many, this may seem a disorienting and disrupting time for the church. We are having to navigate unfamiliar terrain without a clear map. However, change is essential for the continuation of any entity, the church notwithstanding. The biblical imagery of the church is a "community on the move." As the German theologian Jürgen Moltmann so eloquently championed, change is the way God most often does God's work. As we venture forth into this new world, the Psalmist's words serve as our best guide: "Blessed are those who have set their hearts on pilgrimage."

# 2

# Midwives of a New World

## Shane Claiborne

WHILE WE'RE ALL tired of thinking about the pandemic, exhausted by quarantine regulations, overwhelmed with grief over the loss of life, and ready to live in a post-coronavirus world . . . there are some takeaways from this tumultuous season. After all, God works through the cracks of everything—tyrannical reigns of terror and global pandemics alike—and we have both in America.

There's a passage in Hebrews that speaks of a time of "shaking" so that which is "unshakable may remain."[1] Certainly, the pandemic has shaken us. I grieve the loss of life, especially all the lives that could have been saved here in the U.S. had we had better leadership and

---

1. Hebrews 12:26–29: "At that time his voice shook the earth; but now he has promised, 'Yet once more I will shake not only the earth but also the heaven.' This phrase, 'Yet once more,' indicates the removal of what is shaken—that is, created things—so that what cannot be shaken may remain. Therefore, since we are receiving a kingdom that cannot be shaken, let us give thanks, by which we offer to God an acceptable worship with reverence and awe; for indeed our God is a consuming fire."

more empathy for one another. And yet I also think that this season could be a time where some things that needed to be shaken will fall away—like in a refining fire, or a time of pruning. Our grapevine in the backyard is blooming with thousands of grapes, in part because we prune it each year. Jesus spoke a lot in images like this—pruning and cutting some things back, so that the whole vine can be healthier and more fruitful.

During this time of shaking and pruning, some of our theology may die, and it needs to die. The boxes we put God in are often just too small. Some theology is not big enough to hold a pandemic. It's why we've heard some really bad theology from some very prominent leaders here in the U.S., saying terrible things—like the notion that the pandemic is God's judgment on America. Or they have said that God will protect us, and the test of our faith should be recognizing that we don't need to wear masks; later they, or some who have followed their ideas, have died from Covid. (I will leave aside the irony that many of the folks who say they don't need a mask because of their faith in God's protection still own semiautomatic weapons.)

Theology can be toxic. When a ten-year-old gets raped, and our only answer is "God had this happen for a reason"—that is toxic theology. We need a more robust theology of a God who suffers with us—who was born on the margins and executed on the cross, who knows what it feels like to say "I can't breathe"—as thousands of folks are saying throughout the streets of America. God *is* with us. And that means this time of shaking may bring about a work in which our old politicians, stale rhetoric, and impotent governmental structures will fade away—which is a good thing.

Not only is this a time of shaking and pruning, but it is also a time of revelation. I had a journalist ask me if I believed this was the "apocalypse"—inferring that these may be the "end times," sort of like a zombie apocalypse. But I pointed out that the word "apocalypse" literally means "to unveil," "to reveal," or to "to rip away the veil"—from the Greek *apo-* and *kaluptein*—to uncover . . . like when Toto tears away the curtain around the Wizard of Oz and reveals a little old dude behind it all. And in that sense this apocalyptic moment is a good thing. Perhaps it's why Jesus spoke often of having "eyes to see" and "ears to hear"—we are living in a time in which people are seeing injustice and racism and inequality with new and alarming clarity. Scales are falling from more and more eyes. I've often said that Donald Trump did not change America, he revealed America; perhaps he has hastened the scales falling away. The pandemic is doing the same. In this time of reckoning we are seeing some of America's worst demons surface and manifest themselves in a Legion of ways.

The infection and its death toll have disproportionately impacted our most vulnerable people—people of color, folks who are incarcerated and locked up in detention centers on our border, those who are homeless, and the elderly. It has also revealed that there are many people in power who are not concerned about those whom Christ called "the least of these." As my brother The Reverend William Barber (co-chair of the Poor People's Campaign sweeping our country, even amid the pandemic) has said, "Too many people in power are too comfortable with other people's deaths." We must do better.

The pandemic came to the United States during the season of Lent, when Christians around the world remember the life, death, and resurrection of Jesus during the holy season of penitence before Easter. Often, folks fast from life's pleasures, giving up things like chocolate or technology, in order to ground their spirits in prayer. A friend of mine said the pandemic imposed the "Lent of all Lents"—it was like Lent on steroids. We were forced to give up many of our cherished pleasures in this involuntary fast imposed upon us by the virus. And yet what happens when we fast is, we become more deeply sensitized. When we give up food, we appreciate it all the more. And we gain a deeper sense of solidarity with those whose bellies ache with hunger because of poverty and injustice.

In many ways, the pandemic has set before us a similar opportunity of sensitivity. My hope is that this season of social distancing leaves us with a hunger for community like never before. I think we'll all be glad to step away from Zoom calls and Facebook and be with real people again.

It's important to remember there is a long tradition of social distancing in the history of our faith. Think of those forty years in the wilderness as God was preparing the ancient Israelites to be a holy nation. And, similarly, the forty days in the desert as Jesus was preparing for his own ministry. These periods of isolation can show us who we are and—if we will let them—shape us to be the people we are meant to be.

On the other side of these strange seasons, life may not look the same . . . and that's a good thing. A reporter recently asked me when we will get back to "normal." I thought for a moment and said, "I hope the answer to that is *never*." I later wrote an article pointing out the irony that one of the things stopped by the pandemic here in the U.S. is executions; thanks to the pandemic, we just went through one of the longest periods in American history without executions. We don't want to go back to executing people again. My hope is that the pandemic gives us a new appreciation for life, and a new sensitivity, empathy, for those who are suffering. We don't want to go back to normal.

Normal wasn't working. Normal got us George Floyd, murdered by Minneapolis police. Normal got us 105 days lost to gun violence in the United States. Normal got us 700 people a day dying from poverty . . . *before* the pandemic. The pandemic is an invitation to reimagine the world and to insist that we cannot go back to normal.

Even as this is a time filled with grief and anxiety for many, it is also a time full of imagination, pregnant with hope. There's that passage in Romans (8:22, NIV) that says the whole creation is "groaning as in the pains of childbirth." Paul goes on to say that we ourselves groan with the earth.

Does it not feel as though the world is groaning, that the earth itself ravaged by economic exploitation? The masses in our streets are groaning, "We can't breathe." We call childbirth "labor" for a reason. It involves groaning, weeping, tears, sweat, blood . . . and in the end, new life comes. I think of the words of activist and lawyer Valarie Kaur as she named this present darkness we are in: she raises the question, is this darkness the tomb—or is this the darkness of the womb? In this moment of groaning and pain, I believe a new world is being born. And we get to be the midwives.

# 3

# Looking Ahead

## Lorenzo Lebrija

AT THE TRYTANK Experimental Lab, we are focused on seeking out where the Holy Spirit might be leading God's people. This means that we are generally looking at the current context to try to discern where the trends point, and where the church's role is in that future.

The Covid-19 pandemic was not a surprise. We had been warned, as recently as Bill Gates's 2015 TED Talk, that in a super-connected world, a pandemic was not a question of "if" but rather "when." So, as we look ahead, we believe there are three emergent trends that are likely to endure beyond the pandemic and to shape the post-pandemic world—and three more "inevitables" in our future.

These are the three things likely to remain from this pandemic:

*Digital Church.* In some ways, Covid-19 sped up a journey we have been on to get our churches to have digital offerings. And if our job is to "go make disciples," then this is a good thing. There will now be an expectation that churches have digital church as part of regular ministry. The opportunity presented by this is the possibility of creating true community from those joining us online; the challenge is figuring out how best to do this. Also, we'll need to consider how we integrate those who might *only* join us online into the life and work of our congregations.

*Digital Giving.* It's actually a bit surprising how few congregations offered some way to give online before the pandemic. The good news is that most churches that were not doing so quickly jumped on board as the lockdowns took hold. That's good for two reasons. First, digital giving (when done properly) allows us the opportunity to get people to become regular, steady givers. This will help for those drops when people are not in church for any of many reasons, or the slower summer months. Instead of peaks and valleys, there should now be a more steady flow of revenue. Second, our society will eventually become cashless—and so it makes sense that we provide more ways for people (especially the younger ones) to donate. This is also an opportunity to add more professional elements to our fundraising campaigns.

*Younger People.* An interesting thing happened when church had to go digital because of the pandemic: Young people tuned in. Whether that's because they faced their own possible mortality, or because they realized that the promises of the world (more money, cars, a bigger house, or a better job will all make you happy) were "false" promises, we don't yet know. It might even be that church was now more attractive to them because it became available on their own schedule and in a format with which they are very accustomed. The good news is that we now have data that shows they came. It might also match other research that shows that young people are quite open to the Christian faith. We'll need to consider how we capitalize on this opportunity.

So now, let's look further out a few years. These are the three upcoming "inevitables" headed our way:

*Minority Majority.* In 2045, something amazing will happen in the United States. For the first time, the white population will dip below the 50 percent mark of the overall population. According to the Census Bureau, whites will make up 49.7 percent. Minority groups will outnumber whites in this country (Hispanics 24.6 percent, Blacks 13.1 percent, Asians 7.9 percent, and multiracial at 3.8 percent).[2] In fact, by 2060 one in three U.S. residents will be Hispanic.[3] This shift will mean that the country will be impacted in many ways, not least in cultural forms and expressions—which is where faith resides. For a predominantly white church (90 percent according to Pew),[4] this

---

2. U.S. Census Bureau, "Older People Projected to Outnumber Children for First Time in U.S. History," Press Release, March 13, 2018, https://www.census.gov/newsroom/press-releases/2018/cb18-41-population-projections.html

3. Sandra L. Colby and Jennifer M. Ortman, "Projections of the Size and Composition of the U.S. Population: 2014 to 2060," U.S. Census Bureau, March 2015, https://www.census.gov/content/dam/Census/library/publications/2015/demo/p25-1143.pdf

4. Pew Research Center, "Members of the Episcopal Church," Religious Landscape Study, https://www.pewforum.org/religious-landscape-study/religious-denomination/episcopal-church/

means that we have an opportunity to start now to do more to reach the Hispanic population and invite them to join us.

*Climate Change.* The 2018 National Climate Assessment pulled no punches: climate change has already started to affect our daily lives, and this will only continue to be more so.[5] We already see food prices spike when there is a severe heatwave.[6] What will happen when heat makes certain areas inhospitable to humans and farming? Lack of, and more expensive food means that food insecurity will likely become more prevalent. Storms are getting bigger and more severe; the impact will be more loss of life and property (and insurance will be unavailable). Human health, the economy, quality of life—all will be affected by climate change. How do we prepare, both to serve as Christians and for ourselves as a church? What link might there be between this inevitable and the trend identified above of younger people engaging with the virtual church—an age cohort for whom climate change is the surpassing moral question of their generation?

*Cyborgs and Artificial Intelligence.* Although the term "cyborg" was coined in 1960, it is in the next ten years when we will see their impact. Bob Johansen, a fellow with the Institute for

---

5. U.S. Global Change Research Program, "Fourth National Climate Assessment: Volume II: Impacts, Risks, and Adaptation in the United States," https://nca2018.globalchange.gov/
6. Sybille de La Hamaide, Polina Devitt, and Michael Hogan, "Heatwave Ravages European Fields, Sending Wheat Prices Soaring," Reuters, August 2, 2018, https://www.reuters.com/article/us-europe-wheat-harvest/heatwave-ravages-european-fields-sending-wheat-prices-soaring-idUSKBN1KN0L9

the Future, puts it this way: "In ten years, we're all going to be cyborgs."[7] This doesn't mean robots will be taking over. Rather, being augmented by computers, we humans will be able to do things we have never done before. Already in 2016, the first cyborgs competed in the Olympics. With microchip implants we will be able to have "super minds." And of course, artificial intelligence is already a reality in many parts of our lives. There will need to be a deeper conversation about cyber ethics, human dignity, and more—because like any power, this "super" power can also be used for the wrong purposes. As Dr. Johansen told me, "evil is all over this—but where is the church at the table in Silicon Valley?"

The underlying question, of course, is: What do we do with this knowledge? Do we take these advancements as opportunities and prepare for them—or maybe even capitalize on some of them? Or do we wait, pretend there's nothing there for us to worry about as a church, and then get caught by "surprise" when they happen? With a God who is always making all things new, hopefully the question answers itself.

---

7. Bob Johansen, "Faith in the Future," TryTank Webinar, Lecture, June 19, 2020. See also Moises Velasquez-Manoff, "The Brain Implants That Could Change Humanity," *New York Times,* August 30, 2020, SR4, accessed at https://www.nytimes.com/2020/08/28/opinion/sunday/brain-machine -artificial-intelligence.html

# 4

# Sacramental in Action— and Being

## Greg Garrett

IN TIMES OF great disaster, spiritual needs multiply. We need comfort, we need a sense of security and meaning; even our most basic needs, whether for food or shelter or useful engagement, we suddenly see in a different light. And in times when we can't gather in person, those needs become yet more complicated. What the church can bring us in these times is a way of being, a way of thinking, and the very real sense that we are still ecclesia, a community gathered around something much, much larger than ourselves—even if we're separated from some of the formal ways we experience God and revelation.

*What does the church teach us about how to be?* The Anglican tradition offers us a spiritual practice. During the months my family and I were in quarantine, I was grateful for the *Book of Common Prayer*, for the opportunity, if I chose, to structure my day in ways I hadn't since seminary. I wish more people were aware of it; I would not have been without seminary training and study of the BCP tradition. That's too bad, because I need it! I don't meditate—I'm not even very good at sitting still, even after all these weeks—but I can read and I can pray, joining my prayers with the saints across the world and across the ages. The BCP is a vital resource in times of distance, and its presence on my bookshelf was a reminder that I belong to a tradition of prayer and common worship—even if the common part had to be left out. How can the church direct our attention to our life of prayer?

*What does the church teach us about how to think?* I have had too much time to read, watch, and listen, too much time left in my own head, and not all of that thinking was healthy for me. I've had to shut off the firehose of news at some points and become more selective about what I consumed. I've also had to remember what the church teaches about how to respond to human events. I've had to remember that I am called to compassion and not to simple rage, which is where some of each day's headlines daily tempted me. And I've had to remind myself that we discern in community, and that being alone in my own head was bad for me emotionally and spiritually. Remembering that, I reached out to people around the world in the ways left to us—Zoom meetings and FaceTime calls, email, social media. We talked about what we were thinking, and sometimes we encouraged each other to think differently.

*What does the church teach us about community?* It was in those virtual communities and in my family that I found comfort and understanding. Like many introverts, I don't normally gravitate to large gatherings, but I found I missed being in formal worship more and more, and that I needed to create community in any way I could. Although I am not a joiner, I joined Dean Lucinda Laird and congregants at the American Cathedral in Paris for several weeks of lectionary study, and although I never really warmed to online worship,

I tuned in to see friends preach and celebrate. One week I offered the sermon I was supposed to have preached in Paris from my living room, and relished my faith community's comments on the service from six thousand miles away. And perhaps there is a lesson for the church here: I felt most connected online to those with whom I already felt connected, and least with those who didn't share a personal history with me.

*What does the church teach us about the sacraments?* I have, as of this writing, not taken the Eucharist in over three months, the longest period since I came back to faith twenty years ago, and I miss it like sunlight. If there is a pressing question for the church to take up, it is perhaps this one, prompted by my previous thought about connection and personal history. I've read esoteric theological arguments about what can and can't be consecrated, about how far a priest's eucharistic intention might stretch, about whether bread that I as a layperson set on a table while watching a Eucharist on my computer partakes of Real Presence or is an Agape Meal. I know that Presiding Bishop Curry encouraged churches to offer services of prayer rather than solo Eucharists.

But my larger question is this: If the church cannot offer the formal sacraments during times of isolation and distancing, *how can it still offer us sacraments?* Can it teach us to be sacramental in, and think sacramentally about, our lives alone? Can it help us understand the sacramental in the human touch and whatever community is available? Greg Rickel (now the bishop of the Episcopal Diocese of Olympia) quoted Rumi in the first Episcopal sermon I ever heard: "Let the beauty we love be what we do. There are hundreds of ways to kneel and kiss the ground." If the church can help prepare us to kneel and kiss the ground in times of plenty and in times of famine, it will have done its own work hundreds of times over.

21

# Second Conversation: Liturgy and Longing

*What have we learned about the worship we have been offering from having to create new ways of worship? Are there ideas or themes we should be careful not to lose?*

Lizette Larson-Miller, Andrew B. McGowan,
and Deanna Thompson

5

# "Come, Let Us Worship!"

## Lizette Larson-Miller

EARLY IN THE onset of the lockdowns, as churches were struggling to figure out how to respond, Bishop John Taylor of Los Angeles said to his clergy: "In recovering what we love, we should be sure to claim all we have learned." He reminds us that while we longed to return to the fullness of liturgical gatherings, we were given the gift to reflect in exile. Of many possible lessons, we were invited to theologically remember that "matter matters"[8] in distinguishing between worship and liturgy, as well as between sacraments and prayer. From my perspective, two lessons in particular seem to emerge.

Lesson one: Worship of God is a lifestyle; liturgy is *one way* to worship. In other words, worship is the umbrella term, liturgy a subset. Worship in its fullness is "the orientation of all forms of

---

8. Drawing on Geoffrey Rowell, "The Significance of Sacramentality" in *The Gestures of God: Explorations in Sacramentality* (London: Continuum, 2004), 4.

human activity, including the liturgical or ritual, toward a particular allegiance."[9] The pandemic has, in a deep way, "invited" us to remember that worship is everything we do in our lives. While we hungered for the gathered church, especially for our sacramental heart, many Christians expressed in social media and elsewhere that they learned much of worshiping God in other ways, including how to pray. They experienced something of the breadth of the riches of Christian tradition in the liturgy of the hours, devotional prayers, ritual practices, and the contemplative focus that can be found in domestic altars anchored by icons, statues, and candles.

Those who have always done this may shrug their shoulders, but the numerous comments expressing surprise that things such as morning and evening prayer even existed (and clamoring for Zoom guidance on how to do it) tell us clearly of the limitations (or—let it be said—poor quality) of pastoral catechesis in many communities. Diocesan encouragement for households to pray together without a priest or other "professional" leader, and guidelines for the domestic church to celebrate the important holy days through prayer, have given permission and encouragement to the baptized priesthood of all believers. These practices have helped many gain a sense of being worship-oriented Christians beyond and outside ecclesial liturgical actions, a glimpse of the richness of worship as an all-encompassing stance in the life of a Christian.

A life of worship extended beyond Sunday eucharistic participation has also brought new adherents to the recognition that our

---

9. Andrew B. McGowan, *Ancient Christian Worship: Early Church Practices in Social, Historical, and Theological Perspective* (Grand Rapids, Mich.: Baker, 2014), 4.

lives—flowing from our baptism and from the Eucharist—must lead us to be agents of God's mercy in the world. Acts of social justice are worship of God. In the light of the pandemic, this "worship" has opened eyes and hearts to recognize that "returning to normal" is not a Christian goal. Again, many communities have always known and preached this—in words and actions—but the divisions of race, economics, education, and more have become so unavoidable that the impossibility of "normal" for Christians has sunk into conversations among people who have blissfully ignored reality for decades. Here is a glimpse of the breadth of worship that flows from and toward the liturgical fountain of the Holy Eucharist. As we re-gather for liturgy, how do we continue this eucharistic living in all we do?

Lesson two: We have been given the opportunity to remember the relationship between sacrament and prayer, which is a return to sacramental theology. The prayer of the whole church, whether in the daily office or in spontaneous praying communities, has remained fully prayer in our virtual reality because we profess belief that prayer is efficacious for those near to us and those far off (including prayer bridging the living and the dead). But sacramentality, here expressed in the church's sacraments, is about matter, about embodiment, about presence, rooted in the incarnation.

For Anglicanism, returning to Richard Hooker's emphasis on sacramental relationality based on the life and actions of Jesus Christ reminds us that without the incarnation there is no flesh of Christ, and without this flesh there are no sacraments. Matter, presence, embodiment, materiality—these mark sacramental efficacy. The theological acrobatics around virtual eucharistic celebrations during the pandemic were crafted out of medical necessity and a deep hunger. But the importance of theology was ultimately made manifest in a new emphasis on the goodness of created matter and eschatological hope. All our eucharistic celebrations are about real presence and real absence, never complete here and now.

Our season of rehearsed eschatological waiting for what will be will be complete in God's time. Theological reflection is a form of prayer and part of a life of worship before God. May we claim the lessons.

# 6

# The Old and the New

## Andrew B. McGowan

WE OFTEN ASSUME, like colonists and conquistadors of old, that what we seem to have discovered for ourselves is actually new. Yet in liturgy—and in Christian life generally—there are few things that have not appeared before in some form. If we stop and listen to those who were there before us, trying to negotiate the challenges and opportunities about how common life and worship and private lives and spaces relate, we may find our enthusiasm for or fear of these new places tempered, and experimentation or innovation enriched by tradition.

While there are often new technologies, the question of being together "virtually"—"in power" or "in effect"—is as old as liturgy itself. Christian communities have always gone back and forth between the physical gathering and a sense of corporate unity that persists despite separation. And there have been times when the possibilities of being connected in spirit have distracted from the other pole of physical communion.

## Together and Apart

Many churches in recent decades have placed such emphasis on their gathered lives, and less on the vocation and "worship" that takes place in daily life when we are not in the same place, to the point that there is a loss of the necessary reference points to allow us to negotiate each on its own terms. The absence of one through necessity seems to shift the balance to the other. Can we make the life of the individual or the household into church, or vice versa?

The idea that we can and do share prayerfully in a kind of communion even when not gathered is old news. Scripture constantly affirms it, but always also asks where the concrete and material will play their part. One liturgical example in the tradition is of Christian daily prayer, which is as old as eucharistic worship and has had both private and public forms for as long as we know. The Prayer Book offers a form which can serve both purposes, and we have always said the Office together "with" those not physically present with us.

Likewise, eucharistic worship has always been understood to take place "with" many not present in body, so the idea that this is a new or recent possibility should be neatly but firmly put aside. The real question is what part the physical gathering of a community plays when we become conscious in a deeper way of how communion is more than Eucharist.

Our misconception in the present moment may be that what is now a less familiar mode of inhabiting the private and domestic as Christian space, the life given uninvited by the pandemic (but which is familiar to many differently abled or differently resourced), has to be shaped fully in imitation of what we know of the gathered and corporate. Why not have communion while apart? We do. That is not the question; the question is why not call our being apart "being together"?

## By the Book

Technology changes how we negotiate this distinction of communal and private, but does not remove it. The arrival of the printed mass-produced book, in its time just as disruptive a liturgical technology as Zoom, provides a case in point. With an English Bible and common liturgy "understanded of the people" available after the Reformation, many things changed remarkably for English Christians. Anglicans then and since could share various liturgies virtually and domestically, given that words of common prayer and imaginations together provide more than enough to join in spirit with those far away.

At no point however was there a claim that the book made the gathering itself redundant—except of course in communities that placed themselves outside catholic tradition by doing so. Fundamentalist churches are the obvious case in point, with Bible rather than Prayer Book the technological cart placed before the ecclesial horse. The results are all too evident in their fragmentation, and in a basic confusion of the genuinely personal and the purely individual. Instead Anglicans used the book(s) to enhance their private devotions and to claim a sense of spiritual unity, but never to replace the physical gatherings of community with this early modern virtual reality.

## Local and Virtual in Corinth

The issue is actually much older still. The oldest Christian account of a struggle between how private and communal relate in eucharistic worship is found in Paul's correspondence with the Corinthians. The key chapter of his eucharistic discussion refers constantly to gathering, "coming together" (five times), and "to the one place" (11:20; cf. Acts 2:44). Paul does not imagine these meetings are the whole of their Christian life, or that they have no unity or sharing otherwise; but these events are an irreducible element, for reasons that include how the private and the communal had to relate.

The gathering in Corinth was strained to breaking point because it became the venue for display of private difference and distinction (probably even down to the foods being brought and shared) rather than an act that created unity. "Do you not have homes to eat and drink in?" Paul asks (cf. 1 Corinthians 11:22). So there were times to eat separately and, as in all things, to do so in a holy way; but to celebrate this meal required suspending personal and domestic identity in physical acts of sharing.

Paul is clearly interested in the private devotional lives of his readers, and insists that "communion" as a property of Christian life extends beyond the gathering; but eating one loaf and drinking one cup (1 Corinthians 10:16–17) were irreducible material signs of a unity that should then define us, even when apart. Some pretended to create their spiritual progress without one another ("Already you have become . . . kings!" [1 Corinthians 4:8]), even while doubtless proclaiming some form of spiritual unity. The physical meal was a necessary corrective to the ways the privileged tended to work their own spiritual progress out at the pace that suited them.

## Better Together

Imitating the physical gathering privately in ritual terms (whether with book or internet makes little difference)—to the point of claiming that not a virtual but a real Eucharist can be celebrated when apart—misunderstands the place of the gathering. Sometimes there are gifts not available to us, and the Eucharist has been one of these in many cases. Book and imagination and internet all assist us to live into our communion, even when we cannot take communion; but just as there are things only an incarnate savior can do, with all the limits that history imposes, so too there are things that only the Eucharist will bring us.

7

# Our Bodies, Christ's Body, and Virtual Worship in the Time of Pandemic

## Deanna Thompson

WITH MASS MIGRATION to virtual worship, churches across the globe are confronting a host of questions about how and whether key elements of worship can be carried out in virtual spaces. Leaders of several mainline denominations have recommended that while we can't gather in person, communities of faith should refrain from offering communion. Some church leaders have proposed that temporarily foregoing the sacrament allows us to focus renewed energy on how the Word of God comes to us. Those who advocate for no communion via online worship emphasize that faith is not in jeopardy when we don't have access to the sacrament. God's Word is sufficient for the nourishing of faith, they say, an important point that is no doubt comforting to many in this time when access to the sacrament is mostly non-existent.

While it is valuable to stress the sufficiency of the Word for nourishing faith, the fact that Christianity is an incarnational religion means that we also emphasize how God comes close to us through actual material elements like bread and wine.

One of the main reasons for counseling against the practice of virtual communion seems rooted in the conviction that virtual gatherings do not qualify as real gatherings. Those who counsel against providing communion at this time of physical distancing say, "We should wait for communion until we can gather again"—suggesting, of course, that our current gatherings virtually for worship, for evening prayer, for Bible study or youth group differ in essential ways from the times we're physically together.

This time of pandemic offers scholars, theologians, and clergy unprecedented opportunities to reflect more deeply on what being present to one another in virtual spaces actually means. While conventional wisdom tends to view virtual spaces as disembodied and therefore inferior to embodied, in-person presence, theologian Kathryn Reklis insists that our theology must move beyond "seeing the real versus virtual divide in terms of embodied versus disembodied," and argues that we must think more creatively about "the new permutations of digital and virtual technology informing our lives as particular ways we are embodied."[10]

During the past several months of participating in online worship, I have heard many testimonies of others' embodied responses to being part of such worship experiences. Some have fallen to their knees in their living rooms during the prayers of the people; others have marched around their house waving their palms during Palm

10. Kathryn Reklis, "X Reality and the Incarnation," New Media Project, May 10, 2012, https://research.library.fordham.edu/theology_facultypubs/12/

Sunday services; still others find tears running down their cheeks during the hymns and special music church members are providing during the pandemic. For many of us, participating in online services has offered real experiences of gathering, connection, and worship.

If we take seriously that our bodies are involved and engaged in worship streamed through our computers, I think it's possible to affirm that we are "assembled" in an embodied way, even during this time of pandemic. And if we take seriously that we're embodied even when we're gathered virtually, it's also possible to interpret virtual communion as an embodied way of connecting to the real, bodily presence of Christ. Sixteenth-century reformer Martin Luther insisted that "these words ['take and eat, take and drink'], along with eating and drinking are the main things in the sacrament. And whoever believes these words has exactly what they say, forgiveness of sins."[11]

Many Christians understand the sacrament of Holy Communion as a means of grace that nourishes and strengthens our faith for life and ministry in the world. Communion is a ritual that draws us into a longing for God's justice to find its place among us. It empowers us to hope in the coming resurrection and new life. At a time when physical contact is so limited, communing together virtually with our faith communities can affirm the reality that our bodies are engaged in worship even when we're participating from our living room, that we're still connected to the other bodies gathered virtually for worship even when we can only see photos of them online, and that Christ comes to us in the gifts of bread and wine even when our pastor's setting of and inviting us to the table is mediated by a screen.

---

11. Martin Luther, *The Small Catechism* (St. Louis: Concordia Publishing House, 1986), accessed August 21, 2020, https://www.bookofconcord.org /smallcatechism.php

# Third Conversation: Hard Choices and Helping Hands

*What questions about financial structures and sustainability will emerge from this time of isolation to confront parishes and judicatories? Is self-help the only option?*

Elise Erikson Barrett, Miguel Escobar, and James Murphy

# 8

# Working Together as the Way

## Elise Erikson Barrett

IF THERE IS any generalization to be made about the ways in which this time is affecting parishes and judicatories, it is that almost no generalizations can legitimately be made. As we listen to our leaders, they are sharing a range of impressions as diverse as the organizations and bodies they serve. Some of them are finding that while giving is down, so are expenses, so the financial outcome is largely stable. Some are finding that givers are highly motivated, and that their congregations are discovering new senses of purpose and vocation, so finances are strong. Some have good reason to fear that they may not survive this time.

All of them are experiencing deep levels of fatigue as this time of crisis and uncertainty lengthens.

We have observed that the Covid-19 crisis has acted, as one grantee put it, as a "force accelerant," turbo-charging existing trajectories by a decade or more. It has also been an agent of the apocalyptic, uncovering inequities in access to capital and resources that have been present in our structures all along. Given these impacts, we might note the following questions about financial structure and sustainability for the post-Covid church:

1. *Can pastoral leaders and lay leaders work together to address finances (both the pastoral leader's and the congregation's) with mutual vulnerability and love for the mission of their church?* Over and over, we have observed the paralyzing, resentment-building impact of what we have come to call "the culture of shame and blame" around finances. Good pastors often hide financial trouble or insecurity, knowing that their congregants are stressed and struggling; congregation members often assume that pastors have education paid for by "the church" and don't see the complexity of taxes and housing with which pastors must work. We have seen profound transformation when pastoral leaders and lay leaders enter into this space with safety, mutual vulnerability, and commitment to one another. On the other side of the present crises, this courageous move will be more important than ever, as pressing questions about the ability of the church to support a full-time salary, the understanding of the congregation's mission, and the nature of giving are certain to arise.

2. *Can congregations and their regional or governing bodies work together to make hard decisions with open communication and mutual care?* Churches and judicatories too often feel as if they are competing for scarce dollars, and pastors can feel like yet another underappreciated asset on the denomination's balance sheet. We have watched organizations in which judicatories or denominations are investing care and time into the financial wellbeing of their clergy experience shifts, with pastoral leaders testifying, "I never thought my judicatory cared about me.

This changes how I feel about ministry." Mutual tending in systems under extreme stress is more than difficult, but judicatories that can walk with their congregations and pastors will discover more hopeful paths than those that focus exclusively on institutional preservation.

3. *Can seminaries and denominations/equipping and ordaining bodies work together to care for the pastoral leaders in their respective systems?* Theological schools and denominations/judicatories have both been on a trajectory of increased financial stress; this is likely to get pressurized. Nonetheless, can leaders of these institutions work in partnership with one another for the sake of the pastoral leaders in their care, and the churches those pastoral leaders serve? More pointedly, perhaps, can they work together to reimagine the training of a rising generation of pastoral leaders for a changing church?

4. *Can resourced congregations and under-resourced congregations within a denomination or judicatory or community be in this work together?* Pastoral leaders and congregations simply must ask themselves: "How do the existing conditions of inequity and historic under-resourcing that the pandemic has unmasked relate to our congregation/parish/judicatory?" This is, among other important changes, a concrete consequence of the rising realization of how systemic racism has shaped the distribution of resources in our churches. Our initiative's research reminded us years ago that Black pastoral leaders and other pastoral leaders of color, pastoral leaders serving rural congregations, and female pastoral leaders were suffering most from, and are most vulnerable to, economic challenges. This is an opportunity to

take a painful look at these realities and to ask God—and our neighbor—what the next right action step might be.

Self-help, then, is not a viable option. The post-Covid church will have to invest in challenging, hopeful partnerships at all levels if it is to embrace the possibilities created by this time of rupture and uncertainty.

9

# Is Self-Help the Only Option?
# It Must Not Be

## Miguel Escobar

AN ECONOMIC TRAGEDY is unfolding across the United States. On May 6, *The New York Times* reported that the unemployment rate had reached 14.7 percent, the highest since the Great Depression.[12] The Pew Research Center has found that the sudden loss of jobs is especially hitting lower-income communities of color.[13] In New York, the city where I live, soup kitchens and food banks are now reporting record numbers; a volunteer at just one site in the Bronx shared

---

12. Nelson D. Schwartz, Ben Casselman, and Ella Koeze, "How High Is Unemployment? Literally Off the Charts," *The New York Times*, May 8, 2020, https://www.nytimes.com/interactive/2020/05/08/business/economy/april-jobs-report.html

13. Kim Parker, Juliana Menasce Horowitz, and Anna Brown, "About Half of Lower-Income Americans Report Household Job or Wage Loss Due to Covid-19," Pew Research Center, April 21, 2020, https://www.pewsocialtrends.org/2020/04/21/about-half-of-lower-income-americans-report-household-job-or-wage-loss-due-to-covid-19/

that one thousand people had showed up one weekend, and then seven hundred for two weekends in a row. There are profound disparities in terms of who is bearing the brunt of the economic fallout of Covid-19, and such differences are reflected in our congregations.

Amidst all this, I was asked to reflect on what Covid-19 is revealing about the financial structures and sustainability of congregations and judicatories in the Episcopal Church. More specifically, I am to reply to the provocative question of, *Is self-help the only option?*

"Self-help" is the opposite of a faithful approach in times like these.

Even as Episcopal churches struggle against the generations of systemic racism which have resulted in churches with widely varying levels of resources, we can also draw on examples from the first to fourth centuries wherein Christians saw themselves as one part of a larger church body, and pulled together to aid the hardest-hit assemblies and individuals in their communities during times of disaster.

Rather than self-help and financial isolation, financial interconnectedness is in our DNA.

## Jerusalem Collections for Today

In his letters from the middle of the first century, Paul makes multiple references to a Jerusalem Collection: "At present, however, I am going to Jerusalem in a ministry to the saints; for Macedonia and Achaia have been pleased to share their resources with the poor among the saints at Jerusalem."[14] This collection is understood to have been both an expression of unity among the first-century assemblies and as a concrete way

---

14. Romans 15:26; see also 1 Corinthians 16:3; 2 Corinthians 8:14; cf. Galatians 2:10.

of helping the "poor among the saints" of the Jerusalem assembly who were experiencing famine and food shortages at that time.

In every diocese, there are congregations that are being especially devastated by infection, mortality, and unemployment. Within New York, Episcopal churches in the Bronx have been particularly hard hit.[15] In addition to emergency relief grants—such as the Diocesan Emergency Grant program launched by the Episcopal Diocese of New York—what would it look like for a diocesan-wide Jerusalem Collection to support the "poor among the saints" of the Bronx? The Navajo Nation is eclipsing other states' infection rates and mortality.[16] The partnership between Navajoland and the Diocese of Northern Michigan to establish the Covid-19 Fund and Indigi-Aid Telethon echo Paul's first-century collection on behalf of the hungry in Jerusalem.[17] Episcopal Relief and Development has created a Covid-19 Pandemic Response Fund to enable emergency aid to vulnerable communities both in the U.S. and around the world.[18] These

---

15. Amy Yensi, "Saint Luke's Episcopal Church in the Bronx Has Lost 21 Members to Coronavirus," Spectrum News NY1, May 22, 2020, https://wwwny1.com/nyc/all-boroughs/coronavirus/2020/05/22/st--luke-s-episcopal-church-in-the-bronx-has-lost-21-members-to-coronavirus#

16. Simon Romero, "Checkpoints, Curfews, Airlift: Virus Rips Through Navajo Nation," *The New York Times*, April 10, 2020, http://nytimes.com/2020/04/09/us/coronavirus-navajo-nation.html

17. For the Covid-19 Fund, see https://upepiscopal.org/the-covid-19-crisis-in-the-episcopal-church-in-navajoland/; for the Indigi-Aid telethon, see https://www.facebook.com/events/256773012190381/

18. See https://www.episcopalrelief.org/press-resources/press-releases/2020-press-releases/episcopal-relief-development-responds-to-the-covid-19-pandemic/

are all examples of modern-day Jerusalem Collections; there is much, much more we might do.

## Presider as Guardian of All in Need

In his *First Apology*, written around 155 CE, Justin Martyr includes a striking outline of how second-century Christians assembled for worship. Beginning with "Those who have the means help all those who are in want," he describes a threefold order of worship that moves from word to table to collection for the poor. This weekly collection for the poor is given to the presider who "aids orphans and widows, those who are in want through disease or through another cause, those who are in prison, and foreigners who are sojourning here. In short, the presider is a guardian to all those who are in need."[19]

While many congregations in our dioceses have been inconvenienced by Covid-19, some congregations have been devastated by this pandemic. Clergy in these communities are on the frontlines of providing monies to parishioners who are struggling to pay rent, buy groceries, or avoid reliance on payday loans. We should be unafraid to dust off the tradition of a weekly collection for the poor. Well-resourced parishes can follow the example of churches like the Church of the Heavenly Rest, which created a Fund for the Not Forgotten for those who are ineligible for federal assistance (undocumented immigrants, asylum seekers, workers in the gig economy, the formerly

---

19. Justin Martyr's 1 Apology 67 as translated by Gordon Lathrup in *Holy Things: A Liturgical Theology* (Minneapolis: Fortress Press, 1998), 45.

incarcerated).[20] Importantly, a portion of these funds is also going to support congregations in East Harlem.

## Bishop As "Lover of the Poor"

One striking development from the fourth century is that of a bishop's public role as "lover of the poor."[21] Pre-Constantine, aid for the poor had focused primarily on those *within* the Christian assemblies. One of the earliest post-Constantinian understandings of a bishop's public role was as one who lifted up the suffering of the poor—both Christian and non-Christian alike—to a public that was reluctant to confront these matters. This new role was particularly embraced by Basil of Caesarea who, in the wake of a devastating famine in 369 CE, preached forcefully to the wealthy of the city, laying bare the invisible suffering of the poor in vivid terms. His preaching raised money for a soup kitchen to feed the most vulnerable; later, building on this work, he founded what is considered one of the first hospitals, the Basiliad.[22]

Even in our secular age, bishops and other prominent faith leaders command attention through their pulpits, pastoral letters, social media, in letters to the editor, and more. David Bailey, the bishop of

20. See https://www.heavenlyrest.org/not-forgotten

21. Peter Brown, *Poverty and Leadership in the Later Roman Empire* (Lebanon, NH: University Press of New England, 2002), 8. I've also written about the evolution of "bishop as lover of the poor" on my Wealth & Poverty in Christianity blog at https://wealthandpovertyinchristianity.blogspot.com/2020/04/basil-of-caesarea.html

22. Thomas Heyne, "Reconstructing the World's First Hospital: The Basiliad," *Hektoen International*, Spring 2015, https://hekint.org/2017/02/24/reconstructing-the-worlds-first-hospital-the-basiliad/

Navajoland, recently said in an interview with Dean Kelly Brown Douglas of the Episcopal Divinity School at Union Seminary that now is the time for faith leaders to make visible the hidden suffering of those rendered invisible.[23] It's inspiring to see new bishops, like Bonnie Perry of the Diocese of Michigan, raising money for food aid as one of the first acts of her episcopate.[24] They stand in a long line of bishops like Basil of Caesarea.

## Economic Alternatives

As a fourth-century contemporary of Basil, Ambrose of Milan spoke out forcefully against the money-lenders of his city for predatory lending practices, the charging of exorbitant interest rates on loans to people in desperate situations.[25] Tragically, predatory lending remains with us today; in 2016 the *average* interest on a payday loan in South Dakota was 652 percent.[26] With unemployment now as high as it was in the Great Depression, some in our congregations are looking for ways to make ends meet, and predatory lenders are circling above. What is the church's role in condemning predatory lending and offering alternatives?

---

23. See https://www.facebook.com/watch/live/?v=241658956908503&ref= watch_permalink

24. See https://www.facebook.com/bonnieaperry/videos/10223027090726 358/

25. Ambrose of Milan's homily "On Naboth" and his exegetical work "On Tobit."

26. Daniel Moattar, "Trump to Payday Lenders: Let's Rip America Off Again," *Mother Jones*, February 11, 2020, https://www.motherjones.com/politics/2020 /02/trump-payday-loan-bank-rule/

In the wake of the Rodney King riots, Dr. Gloria Brown—then a member of the staff of the Episcopal Church—led an effort by the Diocese of Los Angeles, with support from Episcopal Relief and Development, to establish the Episcopal Community Federal Credit Union (ECFCU) to help devastated communities avoid the payday loan and pawn shops that were the only lenders left as major banks abandoned the hardest-hit areas of the city. Nearly thirty years later, this credit union is proving to be a bulwark against the economic impacts of Covid-19. It is still offering low-interest, small loans to struggling families; at the end of March, as the lockdowns took hold, ECFCU announced an emergency cash fund for churches whose cash flow has dropped, as well as a 50 percent reduction in their customary interest rate for congregational loans.[27]

This diocesan credit union brings me to my final point and a deeply held belief: focusing on economic justice is not only the moral thing to do, it also fosters financial sustainability in the long run. The Episcopal Church runs the risk of losing our moral calling— our saltiness—if and when our wealthiest churches and dioceses self-isolate and neglect the most vulnerable. Now is the time to be remembering our long history of financial interconnectedness, of building relationships across economic divides, holding before us the example of how, time and time again, the early church was a "guardian to all in need."

---

27. Jennifer Miramontes, "Credit Unions for Economic Justice," Episcopal Church Foundation Vital Practices, March 2020; https://www.ecfvp.org /vestry-papers/article/832/credit-unions-for-economic-justice

## Possible Short-Term and Long-Term Actions

### *Short Term*

- Support organizations doing both U.S. and international Covid-19 relief work, such as Episcopal Relief and Development.
- Imagine what a Jerusalem Collection would look like today both at the diocesan and churchwide level. See Navajoland and the Episcopal Diocese of Northern Michigan's Indigi-Aid virtual telethon as a cross-diocesan approach.
- Follow Justin Martyr's example by taking a second collection at services specifically for aid to the poor. See the Church of the Heavenly Rest's Fund for the Not Forgotten as a model for how one well-resourced parish is focusing funding on the most vulnerable.

### *Long Term*

- Recenter in the life of the church the fourth-century expectation that bishops embody the role of "lovers of the poor." This means encouraging the public-facing, moral leadership that leverages the platform and teaching ministries of bishops to highlight the experiences of the most vulnerable—and to raise funds to address urgent need. Urge your bishop to do this boldly.
- Create an Episcopal Church working group to explore models of churchwide credit unions, which have consistently been shown to make communities more resilient in times of economic crisis, including natural disasters.

10

# Avoidance Is No Longer an Option

## James Murphy

PRIOR TO THE elimination of most in-person religious gatherings in March of 2020, numerous parishes and their judicatories (dioceses) struggled greatly with meeting expenses in the face of shrinking congregations and the continued demand of maintaining aging buildings—all while adapting to evolving technology. This year's disruption in income, economic uncertainty, and increased market volatility will force deep discernment at both struggling parishes and those with more assets to ask the following questions, which can no longer be avoided.

### 1. Are parishes doing everything possible to support their mission financially?

If they have not already, parishes must look beyond the simplicity of the weekly offering plate and promote more current ways to accept gifts and diversify income streams. There is no longer time to hesitate on setting up online giving, especially since low-cost software is often available through judicatories. Like other nonprofits, parishes also need to encourage donors to give in new ways, such as popular options like donor-advised fund grants or Qualified Charitable Distributions from IRAs from retirees; and parishes will need to set up brokerage accounts to accept appreciated securities when that suits a willing donor. Parishes that regularly minister to those outside the congregation should consider reaching into the wider communities they serve for financial support. Many who love volunteering for soup kitchens or mentoring programs may rarely attend services, but would support those ministries financially if asked, as might various local organizations/foundations.

Going forward, churches must consider additional income streams beyond regular donations. Creative opportunities should be considered, such as installing cell phone towers inside church steeples or investigating rental opportunities beyond the parish community to make the fullest use of facilities. Parishes should also focus on growing endowments and other invested funds to create more reliable income streams for future ministry. With the huge number of Baby Boomers retiring and generational wealth transfers taking place, now is a clear opportunity for church leaders to build up trust and confidence in visionary, future-focused ministries that inspire donors to make significant gifts, especially planned gifts from their estates. Every parish should do this work even if it is perceived that they lack wealthy donors, as substantial estate gifts often come from those of modest means.

## 2. What new collaborations will enhance ministry and financial sustainability?

Parish ministries could be even more impactful and financially efficient through innovative collaborations with other congregations and organizations. Many parishes seek to fulfill God's call to serve others through various ministries such as feeding programs, youth mentoring, or homeless ministry. Parishes will struggle more now to support those efforts if relying only on parish resources. If parishes collaborate with other congregations or nonprofits doing the same work, they could build more impactful and sustainable programs and reduce expenses. For example, several churches could sponsor a joint food bank—housed at one congregation with the best facility and location for that ministry—while sharing expenses and providing volunteers from each parish.

Recent financial challenges may also prompt judicatories to collaborate more deliberatively. Certainly, some adjacent judicatories should consider merging to eliminate duplication of personnel and administrative costs to serve all parishes more effectively. Other judicatories may continue to exist separately, but could choose opportunities to save expenses by coordinating common vendor contracts for greater discounts, or may discern that certain staff positions could serve more than one judicatory jointly. Cooperating judicatories could also reduce fees by investing endowments together and, through denominational foundation resources, better incorporate socially responsible investment principles across multiple funds. Thoughtful partnerships serve all better.

## 3. Is it time for a parish to evolve into something new?

When new financial resources cannot be found or new collaborations are not feasible, it may be appropriate for a parish to consider more radical options to fulfill its mission and best serve its parishioners. Each situation will be unique, but judicatories can help struggling churches face these difficult realities now, before assets get spent, buildings deteriorate, and terminal choices become imminent. Judicatories should also prompt and guide discernment about proper levels of clergy support at struggling parishes, and help them reimagine what is possible by sharing clergy and other creative options. For some parishes, God's mission may be best served by closing, merging, or evolving into a virtual or home-church community. Strengthening parishes in these imaginative ways will serve the mission of the whole church better. Our time following isolation is the perfect time for reflection and hard questioning as new circumstances, including online ministry, continue to invite deep discernment and truth-telling.

# Fourth Conversation: Inequality, Marginalization— and Renewal

*How can we address constructively the inequality in access to resources within the church laid bare by the variety of responses to the Covid pandemic? What responsibility do well-resourced communities and institutions have in helping poor and marginalized churches keep their communities tended and gathered?*

Kelly Brown Douglas and Molly Baskette

# 11

# The Challenge to the Church during Covid-19

## Kelly Brown Douglas

THAT COMMUNITIES OF color have been disparately impacted by the Covid-19 pandemic has laid bare the ongoing crisis of growing racialized injustice and inequity in this country. This crisis has meant that people of color have been disproportionately susceptible to the realities of poverty—such as lack of housing, health care, and employment. Unfortunately, this social-justice crisis has been long ignored not only by political and civil society, but also by the church. For far too long, the church has neglected the "least of these."

The truth of the matter is racialized oppression and inequality has grown on the watch of those who claim to be church. Hence, calling ourselves church is aspirational. In many respects, therefore, the Covid-19 pandemic has called the church to account. For whether or not we live into the aspiration to be church has much to do with how we respond to those on the underside of justice in this country—to the "disinherited" classes of people like the poor and people of color, those rendered most vulnerable to Covid-19.

And so, while the realities of the Covid crisis have compelled the "church" to focus on the theological appropriateness and spiritual efficacy of "at-home" eucharistic feasts or spiritual communion, we cannot be so focused on eucharistic and other rituals of the church that we forget about the meaning of our gathering in the first place. To do such a thing would be to betray what it means to be church.

For at the center of Holy Communion itself is Jesus's call for *anamnesis*, that is, memorial sacrifice—"Do this in memory of me," Jesus says (Luke 22:19). This call is not a passive process, but rather one in which Christians are invited to enter *into* the sacrifice. It is about being accountable to the past that was Jesus's ministry in the very present. Inasmuch as we are called to gather and come to the altar for communion, therefore we are challenged to go out into the world "remembering" Jesus. Such anamnesis remembrance means nothing less than bringing healing and life-giving justice to the "least of these," hence showing the way toward God's just future as did Jesus.

In the final analysis, we must hear the call of God asking for us to be the church. This is not about returning to a normal that allowed for increasing injustice. Rather, the call of God requires that we move beyond our altars to embody the very ministry of Jesus in our world. It requires that we show up in solidarity with the forgotten poor and subjugated even as we fight for the policies and laws that begin with a concern for those on the underside of justice in this country and world—particularly people of color.

In the words of Episcopal Bishop Barbara Harris, "Church is real when it gets down to the nitty-gritty nub of life where Jesus was in the lives of people." The Covid-19 crisis challenges the church to become "real."

## 12

# Church on Fire

## Molly Baskette

FIVE MONTHS AFTER I arrived as the newly minted senior pastor to my church in Berkeley, California, it burned down. A month later, Donald Trump was elected president. Those two destabilizing events have been the leitmotif of my tenure so far, and have sparked countless other fires: from church conflict over whether or not to replace the smoking carcass of our program building with affordable housing, to disagreements about the best way to confront the white supremacists marking territory in our town square. "Church on Fire," a cheeky adaptation of the Alicia Keys tune, became our theme song.

Now everybody else's church is on fire, too. The twin pandemics of Covid and systemic racism are threatening to undo our faith communities—or remake us. A few years ago I told a room full of pastors that we were entering a time of unprecedented disruption, and that disruption would in fact become our new equilibrium—the only thing we could, in fact, depend upon. I showed them a graph of Moore's law, the exponential growth of technology, superimposed over a graph of human adaptability. It showed that technology surpassed our capacity to absorb change about 2007, the year the iPhone came out. No wonder every new iOS update stresses me out so much.

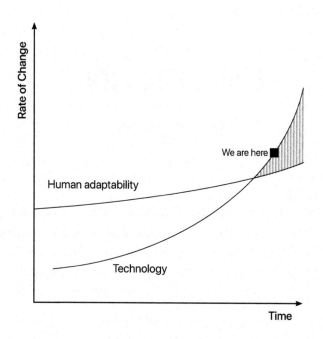

The crosshatch of that graph, where the changes forced upon us meet the upper limits of what we can absorb, is a pain point. It is a cross to bear—and one on which we are borne. We do well to remember that a cross has two axes. The X axis is horizontal: it reaches out to neighbor and kin, it is social, embracing, busy, what my spiritual director sometimes calls "going crazy for the Kingdom of God." The Y axis points both up, our optimistic striving toward God and God's unknown future, and down, grounding and rooting in our ancient story and purpose. It is rooted and rooting, but never rootbound.

Moore's law and the cross both call us to a dynamic stability. How do we hold our center when everything around us is changing? How do we balance innovation and disruption without making ourselves and our communities feel crazy? A friend has embroidered the Beatitudes by adding, "Blessed are the flexible, for they will not get bent out of shape." Dynamic stability is not rigid. It requires the ability to move fluidly from a stable center. Think bike riding, dancing, or surfing, muscles requiring constant recalculation so the body can stay vertical. It takes serious effort and intention at first, but later becomes second nature, as body and mind work together to intuitively adjust to the outside forces acting upon it. Think of Jesus walking on the wild waves of the Sea of Galilee. He didn't just save—he surfed!

Even something as simple as walking is really calculated falling. In this current stormy sea, as we learn to walk again, we can't do things the way we've always done them at church—and thank God for that. The relative quiescence of the church until now might have killed it altogether had not this storm arrived at our doors. It is remaking us, and faster than we ever imagined.

I took advantage of the chaos and disorientation of the church fire to make some sea changes, changes that turned out to serve us exceptionally well when the Bay Area's shelter-in-place order hammered down. I had already replaced our sweet but incompetent A/V guy with a skilled one, commissioned a new and flexible website, and made the initially unpopular decision to herd as many people as possible toward electronic giving. All of this meant we were ready for virtual worship when that became the only option.

Pushing people to change when it wasn't a requirement meant they could adapt more readily when it was. Within a week of the shelter order, we had a creative Mr. Rogers–style variety-show virtual worship, which everyone including our nonagenarians could access, thanks to lay tech helpers in the congregation. We started an All Ages Zoom Story Hour, put pastors' office hours online, organized our congregation into neighborhood pods for mutual aid and to stave off isolation, and invited those with means to give electronically to our Emergency Fund for those who were out of work.

Three months in, the pandemic has impacted us emotionally and substantively; but many, many of my people can't stop citing the blessings and silver linings of this time. They love the creativity and intimacy virtual worship allows (think: talking dogs for Children's Time, and scripture skits done in Legos), and how our Zoom coffee hour breakout rooms are igniting new friendships with people they'd noticed for years and never spoken to. Our worship attendance is up—perhaps doubled or tripled, if we can believe the analytics. We are reoriented enough that we can now address the second, more pervasive and longstanding pandemic: white supremacy and systemic racism, not just out there, but as it works inside our own faith community and in our own souls.

My church may be exceptional (and it certainly has more resources than many), but I doubt it. There is nothing like facing death to make humans realize what really matters and spend more time doing those things: building relationships, finding meaning, singing with gusto, fighting for justice. Reaching out, reaching up, and grounding down.

# Fifth Conversation: Leadership—Challenge and Change

*What has the Covid pandemic taught us about the leaders and structures we have—and the leaders and structures we need?*

Jeffrey D. Lee, Sarah Birmingham Drummond,
C. Andrew Doyle, and Robert C. Wright

13

# Paschal Leaders for a Paschal Church

## Jeffrey D. Lee

*[L]et the whole world see and know that things which were cast down
are being raised up, and things which had grown old are being made
new, and that all things are being brought to their perfection by him
through whom all things were made . . . Jesus Christ our Lord.*
—*Book of Common Prayer*, 291

ABIGAIL NELSON, SENIOR vice president of programs at
Episcopal Relief and Development, frequently reminds members of the board of that organization that epidemics are the great
accelerators—or amplifiers—of realities, trends, flaws, *and* strengths
in cultures and societies across the world. With breathtaking speed,
that reality has now become undeniable in the church. The trends of
institutional decline—particularly evinced by reductions in worship

attendance, financial support, and formal affiliation—are accelerating and/or morphing quickly in this time of pandemic. In a few months' time, most aspects of the observable life of congregations and dioceses have been transformed into primarily a virtual network of Zoom meetings and emails. Even the most optimistic hopes for more effective treatments and vaccines cannot guarantee a return to a pre-pandemic state of "normalcy," for either the institutional church or society in general. The future is here.

In the opening days of this pandemic, quite naturally the most immediate concerns for the church seem to have been questions about public worship. In a church so defined by its observance of sacramental practice, the inability to gather for face-to-face worship raised existential questions. For many clergy leaders, the anxiety was acute. Bishops were besieged with detailed questions from clergy about how the Eucharist might or might not be celebrated. These questions were often driven by profound pastoral concerns for the needs of the Christian people, but they revealed as well a real anxiety about pastoral identity: if we are no longer presiding in the congregation's regular worship, who *are* we?

The questions and concerns continue. Experiments are underway with "virtual" celebrations of the Eucharist, drive-in worship, remote deliveries of Holy Communion, and so forth. In many ways, though, I believe these technical questions are revealing the real and fundamental question of just who and what the church is.

And that question is the heart of the discernment that must be exercised now about the kinds of structures and leadership skills the church must have in order to remain faithful to Christ and even thrive in this new landscape. The bulk of current institutional structures and leadership models we brought with us into the pandemic will simply not be sustainable for long, and may even prove to be irrelevant to—or an outright obstacle to successfully adapting for—the post-pandemic church. Twenty years into this century, the church's sense of identity has relied excessively on resource-demanding buildings, lengthy and expensive ordination processes, complicated legislative assemblies, and other trappings appropriate perhaps for a church in the mid-twentieth century, but no longer. Signs of the inadequacy of much of the church's current institutional life have been there for a long time; the pandemic is speeding up precipitously our confrontation with that reality.

The church is the Body of Christ, dying and rising with Christ in the midst of and for the sake of this world God loves so much. That identity is not dependent on any particular institutional structure—throughout history, the visible church has taken shape and been organized in a variety of ways, from small domestic gatherings at odds with the surrounding culture, to being virtually indistinguishable from the imperial state—or, more recently, the commercial firm. Some of those structures seem to have been more transparent to the Paschal character that Paul and early theologians describe as the core identity of the church; others, obviously less so.

The question for our own time has to be what structures and leadership skills will best serve in making real the fundamental character of our identity as living limbs and members of the dying and rising Jesus. Sacraments do not make true; they make real. In Holy Baptism, we are plunged into the death and resurrection of Christ and called together to make that truth real, so that the Paschal Mystery can be experienced, tasted, and touched—the hungry fed, the marginalized lifted up, the dead raised to new life.

We need leaders with fierce clarity about the church's identity in Christ, who are Paschal to their core. We need leaders who know that death is not the final word, who are unafraid of letting go, dismantling structures that no longer serve effectively to make our identity clear—even when that means dismantling the privileges for our leaders traditionally associated with those structures. It is hard to imagine how the church of the early second century could have recognized that church of the fourteenth century, or how the church of the high Middle Ages could grasp that of the mid-twentieth century in all its complexity.

And yet, the very fact of the church's observable presence, from the Day of Pentecost down to this day, might well be seen as a sign of God's relentless determination continually to bring new life out of death. It is time for the church, and for her leaders, to trust as never before that God is bringing all things to their perfection in Jesus Christ.

# 14

# Supply Chains

## Sarah Birmingham Drummond

THE REVEREND JEFFREY BROWN, minister and co-founder of Boston TenPoint Coalition against youth violence, loves to tell the story about his transition out of seminary. When Jeff graduated from Andover Newton, the theological school where I now serve as dean, he was full of fascination. He had learned so much about the Bible, theology, and the rich history of the Christian tradition, and he wanted to share it all. Immediately.

When Jeff became pastor of a historic Baptist congregation in Cambridge, Massachusetts, he had visions of growing it into a mega-church. That did not happen, but the small and aged congregation—which actually shrank during his first year as parishioners died—taught him how to be a minister. After his first sermon, long and complicated and ending with what he called a "Tillichian twist," a grandmother of the church took Jeff aside and gave him advice that changed his life: "You have to put it where people can get it."

During the past two months, I have heard the term "supply chain" more than in all my previous years combined. Supply chain

71

problems plagued the distribution of personal protective equipment for frontline workers fighting Covid-19. Supply chain issues thwart the development and distribution of tests for the virus, as different components needed for test kits come from different parts of the world. Now, supply chains that make food available far from where food is produced are under such strain that farmers are culling cows and pouring milk down the drain while families in underserved communities go hungry.

Leaders in every field have to rethink supply chains right now. Christian ministers and lay leaders are no exception. The Apostle Paul tells Christians that they must gather together for worship, but he doesn't tell us how. It is faith leaders' responsibility to create new options in every circumstance, in each new generation. During this pandemic, some churches are worshiping online, in drive-ins, over the phone. Others are creating confusion, chaos, and conflict by insisting that communities come together against all public health advice. The debates erupting—social distancing guidelines versus admonitions that Christians must gather—are not theological questions. They are a matter of supply chains.

Jeff Brown got the advice, "Put it where people can get it." The first thing we must ask when reconsidering our work in this strange and unsettling time is, What *is* "it"? We must define what we seek to deliver, and then consider how to deliver it in new ways.

Faith communities deliver comfort and togetherness. They also deliver challenges to think in novel ways, sometimes ways that run counter to what the secular market economy tries to convince us is true. Faith community leaders would be better served by focusing attention, reflection, and conversation on the "it." When we don't do the work of clarifying what faith communities actually are and need to be, we mistake the cart for the horse—the form for the purpose—and conflict arises. It's only natural that political partisanship would insinuate itself into the fissures of division.

The great rethink that Covid-19 is requiring of us is going to change the church forever, for bells are ringing that cannot be un-rung. One of those bells is the realization on the part of faith communities that they have a much bigger toolbox than they realized for carrying out the "it" that is church. Now that people know what it feels like to have their churches "put it where they can get it," they will expect that new supply chain to continue. At first, it is possible—even likely—that these expectations will overwhelm religious leaders, but like Jeff, we will adapt, and the initial strains will have been worth it. We must alter our supply chains, because it is the message, and not its logistics, that matters to the mission of God. Said in a different metaphor, the purpose of our field of mission is not to pasture our sacred cows.

For Jesus tells us, "you will know the truth, and the truth will make you free" (John 8:32). The truth is not a delivery system. Rather, the delivery system *serves* the truth. It is up to religious leaders to focus communities on the truth and then adapt the delivery systems accordingly. This is a big job, but we are not the first to do it. This is not Christianity's first challenge; it's not even our first pandemic.

In each generation we must rethink our supply chains so that God's love might flow even—especially—in hard-to-reach places where it is needed most.

15

# Everything Has Changed?
# Leadership for the
# New Mission Age

## C. Andrew Doyle

IN A CRISIS, amplification and acceleration will fool us into thinking everything is changed. The stresses of Covid-19 have surely obscured our capacity to find clarity; but beyond this, the events of 2020 have left people shaken. These events include partisan political rancor, the loss of work, racial protests following the killings of George Floyd, Breonna Taylor, and Ahmaud Arbery—as well as the pandemic. The reality is that our churches are in a semipermanent state of *apostoli* (or mission—*missio*) rather than *koinonia* (Christian fellowship).[28]

When we stop and think about this volatile, uncertain, complex, and ambiguous world (VUCA),[29] we might realize that our

---

28. A statement made to me by liturgist Paul Roberts of Trinity College, Bristol.
29. "VUCA" is an acronym first used in 1987, drawing on the leadership theories of Warren Bennis and Burt Nanus by the Army War College.

perception is primarily based upon our western, educated, industrial, rich, and democratic lens (WEIRD)[30] lens. Only those with a particular worldview may venture the comment "everything has changed." Why? Globally we have been dealing with Covid viruses since the 1960s. Whole societies around the world have faced similar paralyzing pandemics and epidemics as a constant threat.[31] Our politics have been growing in hostility for over four decades. Black Americans have faced racism, vigilante killing, and denigration by the white public since slavery ended. The precariousness of life and work for the vast majority of the world's population and many Americans is a daily menace.

Currently, the world of virtual interconnectivity has merged the office and home and church into one space. Virtual worship has become the perpetual interim norm. In the midst of this, an

---

30. Joseph Henrich, Steven J. Heine, and Ara Norenzayan, "The Weirdest People in the World?" *Behavioral and Brain Sciences* 33(2–3), 61–83 (2010). See also The Daily Dish, "Western, Educated, Industrialized, Rich, and Democratic," *The Atlantic*, July 18, 2013 http://www.theatlantic.com/daily-dish/archive/2010/10/western-educated-industrialized-rich-and-democratic/181667/ ; and Oliver Burkeman, "This Column Will Change Your Life: Weirdness Just Got Weirder," *The Guardian*, September 17, 2010; http://www.theguardian.com/lifeandstyle/2010/sep/18/change-your-life-weird-burkeman
31. The World Health Organization lists a number of active epidemics and pandemics as of the date of this writing: Chikungunya, Cholera, Crimean-Congo hemorrhagic fever, Ebola virus disease, Hendra virus infection, Influenza (pandemic, seasonal, zoonotic), Lassa fever, Marburg virus disease, Meningitis, MERS-CoV, Monkeypox, Nipah virus infection, Novel corona-virus (2019-nCoV), Plague, Rift Valley fever, SARS, Smallpox, Tularaemia, Yellow fever, and Zika virus disease. See https://www.who.int/emergencies/diseases/en/

awakening has stripped away the veils from our society's ugliest tendencies toward racism and violence. A host of cultural institutions requires reform: health care, the workplace, schools, the police, our political party system, and church. There are a range of options but generally two choices about what to do with this information: a) return to our normal and put blinders on hoping that it won't get this bad again; or, b) wake up and join the mission.

The truth is that Option (a) is not much of an option. The cascading impact of lockdowns, necessary for public health reasons, is slowly grinding our economy to a halt. U.S. banks are on the edge of a breakdown because of corporate debt. The workplace is changed, and the number of jobs will not quickly rebound if corporations can't pay salaries. Profit and nonprofit organizations alike will struggle to reopen—including many churches. The death toll from Covid is growing. Covid will have lasting physical effects on many of its survivors. Institutional change is likely going to take the form of a modification of, and not new thinking about, racism or community accountability. We are seeing the fragmentation of our political party system and growing dissatisfaction by citizens. Meanwhile, we, as a body of Americans, seem unwilling to do the basics—like wearing masks.

If we choose Option (b)—if we choose to awaken and join God's mission—some questions face us. If we decide to lead, we will have to build a collaborative vision to glimpse a horizon higher and more significant than what we see from where we now stand. We, as Christians, will need a theology more substantial than our societal ailment. We must have an understanding of each other. Clarity, not certainty, is essential. Our volatile, uncertain, complex, and ambiguous world eats certainty for lunch. Clarity around organizational opportunities, and theological clarity about God's narrative, creation, and creatures, is no longer optional; it is the necessary condition of our future. Without it we will fail to move from "volatile, uncertain, complex, and ambiguous" to *vision, understanding, clarity, and adaptability*—which is, after all, what faithful people should excel at.[32] Our old structures (police, government, politics, economics, and even the church) are made for an industrialized white world that doesn't exist anymore. Adaptability demands that we move beyond tribal identities. Church leadership must be intentional about shaping this change, or it will suffer as a bystander.

Let me be clear: I am not for terra-forming the society or even the church to make it inhabitable for a new ruling class or limited political ideology. I am interested in God's narrative and its profound message of gospel intervention in a world that has lost its way.

We need to be curious about the following questions:

- Is our theology (sacramental and practical) big enough to engage the virtual world?
- Are we prepared for an excarnational mechanized society of virtual reality?
- Does our theological anthropology have the tensile strength to take on the philosophy of consciousness?
- Is our mission a mission?
- Are we courageous enough to leave our buildings once we return to them?

---

32. This inversion of the VUCA acronym is the inspiration of Bob Johansen. See especially his *The New Leadership Literacies: Thriving in a Future of Extreme Disruption and Distributed Everything* (Oakland, Cal.: Berrett–Koehler, 2017).

- Will we return and lock the doors behind us? Or, will we engage the mission work outside our doors?
- Will we have a missiology audacious enough to share the gospel in an age starkly characterized by the computer-integrated buffered self?
- Will we have a theology of service that is profound enough to see that handouts are a bygone era's way of doing charity?
- Will we be courageous enough to engage real community health, wellness, education systems that work, community policing that is accountable, economic systems that work for all people, political systems that emerge with voices of the minority-majority?
- Will we have an Easter theology that speaks of life after death but has a profound resurrection message for the world in which we live?
- Do we believe in the bodily resurrection? Of ourselves, our churches, and our communities?

The leadership we need must be capable of holding onto these questions while looking to the edge of the church community. Where are the people answering these questions through innovation and creativity? Where are people discovering interesting practical ministry applications in the new mission age? That is where leaders will need to give cover to the voices of clarity and understanding. That is where leaders will need to reinvest resources (human and financial). In those places, at the edge where our discomfort meets the promise of imagination, leaders need to position themselves, moving and stretching their emotional and pastoral capital to provide water, light, and hope where new life is beginning.

## 16

# Authority Is Exerted; Leadership Is Exercised

## Robert Wright

WELCOME TO A giant moment of reflection for our whole society and our whole church. Welcome to this moment of reckoning. Don't be afraid; don't duck; don't just go into the basement until it blows over. Trust me, when you come back upstairs, the whole world is going to be changed. So, what is this telling us about the leaders that we have, and the leaders we need to become?

In my own ministry in the church, I'm excited about finding a growing synergy between the best thinking emerging today from the academy and from practitioners on the nature and practice of leadership, and the teachings of the gospel of Jesus Christ. Not long ago I finished a class at MIT's Sloan School of Management. I found in my studies that I was not being asked to baptize a secular idea and bring it to the church; instead, as I went deeper into the study of leadership, I discovered again and again that Jesus was there first, that his leadership footprints are already there. What we are calling "cutting-edge" leadership theory today, what is selling books in the airport book-stores, is already there in Matthew, Mark, Luke, and John.

Somewhat to my surprise, perhaps, I find in the lexicon I'm gaining from the academy new ways to see the genius of God as lived out by Jesus Christ. When I reflect on the difference between the exertion of formal authority and exercise of authenticity in leadership through the lens of the gospels, I see Jesus actually living it out. I see the Pharisees and the Sadducees absolutely apoplectic when they encounter in Jesus someone who endeavors to (and succeeds in) exercising leadership who is completely without any formal authority to do so. There perplexity is perfectly captured in their question: "By what authority do you say these things?" It is the same as asking: Where did you go to seminary? What family are you from? Jesus is democratizing the idea of leadership—or as the academy would put it, he is exemplifying the idea of nonpositional leadership. He is saying that, at its core, the purpose of exercising leadership has nothing to do with the ego needs of the one who occupies a role and everything to do with helping all people to realize their full potential, period. Exercising leadership is about activity and not role.

That excites me. It also humbles me. It makes me realize that I can actually be a bishop and exert authority and even do it well, yet discover at the end of the day that doing so is not at all the same thing as exerting leadership. So, I spend a lot of time thinking about the overlap between exerting authority and exercising leadership. How do they complement each other—and how are they at odds with each other? What I fear the church has backed herself into, despite protestations to the contrary, is the belief that exerting formal authority—as bishop, priest, or deacon—is the same thing as exercising leadership. Said plainly, it's just not. Authority isn't inherently bad; it isn't inherently good. It is a resource for leadership; but it is not the same thing as leadership.

In God's great mercy it may not be a coincidence that in this moment of the foundations shaking, of our reckoning with our church's own entanglement with racist systems and our nation's profound struggle to manage a public health crisis, we have been reminded again of such examples as C. T. Vivian and John Lewis—who taught us the importance of the distinction between doing leadership and merely relishing authority. Even Jesus pointed to different models of leadership that contrasted with how the Jesus community was supposed to work—those who "lord it over them, and their great ones are tyrants . . . but not so with you" (Matthew 20:25, Luke 22:25). Jesus taught us that leadership, as far as the gospels are concerned, is great; it's first; and its different. Both Lewis and Vivian knew that, taught that, and exemplified it.

So, in this moment we must be willing to interrogate ourselves and the cultures of our institutions and organizations. We must ask ourselves: are we just dithering around with things that are interesting, while avoiding the things that are compelling and transformative? Leadership interrogates the given and seeks the transformative, at least when it corresponds to what Jesus actually teaches.

Think about that in terms of how our church usually works— on any level, in any structure, at any size. This thought haunts me: If the emotional and spiritual maturity will only rise to the level of the people who most often have the microphone, how far will we be able to grow? We treasure our systems of governance; but often the people who most effectively exercise quiet leadership—the leadership of example, the nonpositional leadership of informal authority decentered from formal structures—get effectively silenced. Those folks—the "Israelites in whom there is no guile"—those are the voices we need right now; those are the people whose thinking has not been conditioned by the structures we've created that are now focused primarily on keeping themselves intact.

This means you have to be questioning yourself—not a thing, I confess, I'm naturally or temperamentally inclined to do. It means the leaders we need must be purpose-centered and pretense-free. That's a daunting thought to anyone who ever puts a miter on their head to walk in a procession.

Jesus teaches another leadership lesson, by the example of his ministry—and it's another thing first found in the gospels and now being described, not discovered, by the academy. Jesus is the asker of beautiful questions. He is an interrogator of unique gentleness and deft skill. When he does this—with the concept of the neighbor, with the imagery of the Kingdom of Heaven—he is an artful framer of questions. Many of us in positions of leadership, in the church or elsewhere, get stuck and find ourselves stale because we've made our way by being the answerer of questions. We pride ourselves on our competencies. (I readily admit this is my own tendency.) The leaders we need now are those who reframe the problem and increase energy by crafting and posting catalytic questions. The parables Jesus tells don't offer answers; they often have unsatisfying endings. But that itself is an invitation; the listeners become engaged in the work of imagining their own answers, guided by the imagery of the beautiful question. It is a way of exerting leadership behavior that recruits, and trust partners guided by a shared purpose to run innovations and make progress.

But here is a last thing to consider—perhaps a cautionary tale. A careful reading of Matthew, Mark, Luke, and John tells us that perhaps, in Jesus's childhood, he was very present in the temple. Yet there came a point at some point in his life that Jesus was irregular in his attendance. John finds himself spending his time at the Jordan; Jesus finds himself moving from place to place in Galilee. It may be, of course, that so strong was their formation as young people that they no longer needed to be engaged in the life of temple worship.

But it is also possible—and I think more likely—that the reason was a different one; it was because they were so dissatisfied with the spiritual inertia of the temple that they sensed God's mission was better sought outside its structures, practices, and traditions. They went outside. And wouldn't you just know it—that meant the answers faithful people were asking to the question of where God was calling them into the future was found outside, too.

To engage the gospel, even slowly, is to see that we've taken a particular slant that leaves off the table a lot of opportunities for people to see themselves in the story. I wonder about this in regular diocesan practices. I'm struck by how, especially in these recent months, I've experienced to a greater extent what I can only describe as an invitation, even a hope, that I'll just set out the direction—just articulate the answers. Not only because of Covid, not only because of or reckoning anew with our love affair with racism, but because of our general sense of the church being under siege; we are not just willing, but eager to find the person who will simply give us, even dictate, the answers.

But that is in profound contrast to a gospel-centered practice of constantly interrogating assumptions, interrogating privileges, interrogating structures, and inviting all to take up agency and be a partner with Jesus through the power of the Holy Spirit. That is hard work; and when we exercise that kind of leadership in the midst of our shattered culture, the first response of our people will often be anxiety, complaint, or paralysis. But the exercise of leadership as invitation, leadership as artful questioning, leadership of wider and wider inclusion, leadership as willingness to put mission before institution—that will draw us out of the incarceration of our assumptions and into new imagining and possibility.

# CONTRIBUTORS

**Elise Erikson Barrett** serves as the coordination program director of the Lilly Endowment's National Initiative to Address Economic Challenges Facing Pastoral Leaders. A graduate of Hanover College and Duke Divinity School, she has served in pastoral roles in the United Methodist Church and in leadership positions in the Indiana Philanthropy Alliance. She is the author of *What Was Lost: A Christian Journey Through Miscarriage* (2010).

**Molly Baskette** is the senior minister of First Church Berkeley, California, a congregation of the United Church of Christ. A graduate of Dartmouth and Yale Divinity School, she writes devotional materials for the UCC's Still Speaking Writers Group. She is the co-author of *Real Good Church: How Our Church Came Back from the Dead and Yours Can, Too* (2014); *Standing Naked Before God: The Art of Public Confession* (2015); and *Bless This Mess: A Modern Guide to Faith and Parenting in a Chaotic World* (2019).

**Paul-Gordon Chandler** is rector of the Anglican Church in Qatar (The Church of the Epiphany and The Anglican Centre), and an appointed mission partner of the Episcopal Church. He is the founding president of CARAVAN, an international peacebuilding nonprofit that uses the arts to build sustainable peace around the world. He is the author of several books, including *In Search of a Prophet: A Spiritual Journey with Kahlil Gibran* (2017); *Songs in Waiting: Advent*

*Reflections on Middle Eastern Songs* (2009); and *Pilgrims of Christ on the Muslim Road: Exploring a New Path Between Two Faiths* (2008).

**Shane Claiborne** is the co-founder of Red Letter Christians, a movement to take Jesus seriously by committing to doing first and foremost what Jesus said. An activist, commentator, and frequent speaker, he is the author or co-author of numerous books, including *The Irresistible Revolution: Living as an Ordinary Radical* (2006); *Jesus for President: Politics for Ordinary Radicals*, with Chris Haw (2008); *Enough: Contentment in an Age of Excess*, with Will Samson (2009); *Red Letter Revolution: What If Jesus Really Meant What He Said*, with Tony Campolo (2012); and *How the Death Penalty Killed Jesus and Why It's Killing Us* (2016).

**Kelly Brown Douglas** is dean of the Episcopal Divinity School at Union Theological Seminary, where she holds the Bill and Judith Moyers chair in theology. A graduate of Denison University and Union Theological Seminary, she also serves as canon theologian at Washington National Cathedral, and theologian in residence at Trinity Church Wall Street. Previously on the faculties of Goucher College, Howard University School of Divinity, and Edward Waters College, she is the author of numerous books and articles, including *The Black Christ* (1994); *Sexuality and the Black Church: A Womanist Perspective* (1999); *Black Bodies/Christian Souls* (2005); *Black Bodies and the Black Church: A Blues Slant* (2012); and *Stand Your Ground: Black Bodies and the Justice of God* (2015).

**C. Andrew Doyle** is the ninth bishop of the Episcopal Diocese of Texas. A graduate of the University of North Texas and the Virginia

Theological Seminary, he served parishes in Temple and College Station, and served the diocese as canon to the ordinary before being elected bishop in 2008. He has written a number of books, including *Unabashedly Episcopalian: The Good News of the Episcopal Church* (2012); *A Generous Community: Being Church in a New Missionary Age* (2015); *Small Batch: Local, Organic, and Sustainable Church* (2016); *The Jesus Heist* (2017); and *Vocatio: Imaging a Visible Church* (2018).

**Sarah Birmingham Drummond** is the founding dean of Andover Newton Seminary at Yale Divinity School. A graduate of Yale College, Harvard Divinity School, and the University of Wisconsin, her scholarly interests center on the study, teaching, and execution of administrative leadership in the life of the church. She is the author of *Holy Clarity: The Practice of Planning and Evaluation* (2009); *Leading Change in Campus Religious Life: A Case Study on the Programs for the Theological Exploration of Vocation* (2015); and *Dynamic Discernment: Reason, Emotion, and Power* (2019). She serves as a commissioner for the Association of Theological Schools, and chairs the task force redeveloping ATS's accrediting standards.

**Mark D. W. Edington** (editor) is the bishop in charge of the Convocation of Episcopal Churches in Europe and suffragan for Europe to the Presiding Bishop of the Episcopal Church. A graduate of Harvard Divinity School and the Fletcher School of Law and Diplomacy, he previously served as the senior administrator of the Center for the Study of World Religions at Harvard Divinity School; the founding executive director of the Harvard Decision Science Laboratory; and the director of the Amherst College Press. He is the author of *Bivocational: Returning to the Roots of Ministry* (2018);

and his essays have appeared in *The Atlantic*, *The New York Times*, *Le Monde*, and other outlets. He is a life member of the Council on Foreign Relations.

**Miguel Escobar** is executive director of Anglican studies at the Episcopal Divinity School at Union Theological Seminary. Previously, he served in a variety of senior leadership positions at the Episcopal Church Foundation, including managing program director for leadership and external affairs, and for leadership resources and communications; and senior program director for leadership resources. He also served as a communications assistant to Presiding Bishop Katharine Jefferts Schori.

**Greg Garrett** is a professor of English at Baylor University and theologian in residence at the Cathedral of the Holy Trinity (the "American Cathedral") in Paris. A writer of fiction and a scholar whose research interests are focused at the intersection of religion and culture, his books include *Stories from the Edge: A Theology of Grief* (2008); *Holy Superheroes! Exploring the Sacred in Comics, Graphic Novels, and Film* (expanded edition, 2008); *We Get to Carry Each Other: The Gospel According to U2* (2009); *One Fine Potion: The Literary Magic of Harry Potter* (2010); *The Other Jesus: Rejecting a Religion of Fear for the God of Love* (2011); *Crossing Myself: A Story of Spiritual Rebirth* (2016); *In Conversation: Rowan Williams and Greg Garrett*, with Rowan Williams (2019); and *A Long, Long Way: Hollywood's Unfinished Journey from Racism to Reconciliation* (2020).

**Lizette Larson-Miller** is Huron-Lawson professor of liturgy at Huron University College, part of the University of Western Ontario in London, Ontario. She is also canon precentor of the Diocese of Huron in the Anglican Church of Canada, where she serves on the Worship and Doctrine Commission; and chair of the International Anglican Liturgical Consultation. She has written extensively on liturgical history and theology, particularly on rites with the sick, dying, and dead, including *The Sacrament of the Anointing of the Sick* (2005) and "Dying and Death" in *The Alcuin Guide to the Study of Liturgy and Worship* (2013); on the history of the Eucharist, including "The Liturgical Inheritance of the Late Empire in the Middle Ages" in *A Companion to the Eucharist in the Middle Ages* (2012) and "The Evolution of Eucharistic Practices, 3rd-5th Centuries" in *The Oxford Handbook of Early Christian Ritual* (2017); and on the rites of initiation, including editing the volume *Drenched in Grace: Essays in Baptismal Ecclesiology Inspired by the Work and Ministry of Louis Weil* (2013).

**Lorenzo Lebrija** is the founding director of TryTank Experimental Lab, a research initiative identifying and exploring creative ways to equip future leaders to reinvigorate the church. A graduate of Florida International University and the General Theological Seminary, he previously served as chief development officer for the Episcopal Diocese of Los Angeles; as president and chief executive officer of the Seraphic Fire and Firebird Chamber Orchestra in Miami; and as Miami program director for the John S. and James L. Knight Foundation.

**Jeffrey D. Lee** is the twelfth bishop of the Episcopal Diocese of Chicago. A graduate of the University of Michigan and Nashotah House Seminary, he served as rector of churches in Wisconsin and Washington, church developer, and canon to the ordinary before his election as bishop in 2007. As bishop he has focused the diocese's resources on fostering cultural vitality, overseen the reunification of the dioceses of Quincy and Chicago, overseen significant growth and capacity building in Latino congregations, and helped diocesan leaders to confront the legacy of slavery.

**Andrew B. McGowan** is McFaddin professor of Anglican studies at Yale Divinity School, and dean and president of Berkeley Divinity School at Yale. Prior to this appointment he was warden of Trinity College at the University of Melbourne and Joan F. W. Munro professor of historical theology at Trinity College Theological School, Melbourne, within the University of Divinity. His scholarly interests center on the Eucharist, sacrifice, food, and meals in antiquity; early North African Christianity; and Anglican theology. He serves as the editor of the *Journal of Anglican Studies*. He is the author of numerous articles and books, including *Ascetic Eucharists: Food and Drink in Early Christian Ritual Meals* (1999); *Ancient Christian Worship: Early Church Practices in Social, Historical, and Theological Perspective* (2014); and *Ancient and Modern: Anglican Essays on the Bible, the Church, and the World* (2015).

**James Murphy** is managing program director at the Episcopal Church Foundation (ECF). He oversees ECF's financial development programs and resources, including endowment management, planned giving, and donor solutions initiatives, including ECF's Donor-Advised Fund. He is also general editor and a contributing author for *Faithful Investing: The Power of Decisive Action and Incremental Change*, an ecumenical book on socially responsible investing, and a contributor to *One Minute Stewardship*, both from Church Publishing Inc.

**Deanna Thompson** is director of the Lutheran Center for Faith, Values, and Community and Martin E. Marty Regents Chair in Religion and the Academy at St. Olaf College. As a white Lutheran theologian, Thompson has addressed white privilege and anti-blackness in dominant forms of American Christianity for over twenty years in her writing, speaking in churches on the topics of white privilege and structural racism in American Christianity, and teaching Contemporary African American Religious Thought. She is the author of *Crossing the Divide: Luther, Feminism, and the Cross* (2008); *Hoping for More: Having Cancer, Talking Faith, and Accepting Grace* (2012); *The Virtual Body of Christ in a Suffering World* (2016); and *Glimpsing Resurrection: Trauma, Cancer, and Ministry* (2018). Her 2014 commentary on Deuteronomy for the Westminster John Knox Series, *Belief: A Theological Commentary on the Bible*, was awarded the distinction "Reference Book of the Year" by the Academy of Parish Clergy.

**Robert Wright** is the tenth bishop of the Episcopal Diocese of Atlanta and the first African American to be elected a bishop of the Episcopal Church in Georgia. A former U.S. Navy helicopter crew chief and search-and-rescue diver, he is a graduate of Howard University and the Virginia Theological Seminary, and holds certificates in biblical studies from Ridley Hall, Cambridge University; from the Harvard Summer Leadership Program; and from the Oxford University program in Pastoral Leadership.